CN00660438

THE HISTORY OF 30 ASSAULT UNIT

Ian Fleming's Red Indians

Craig Cabell

Pen & Sword
MILITARY

First published in Great Britain in 2009 by
PEN & SWORD MILITARY
an imprint of
Pen & Sword Books Ltd
47 Church Street
Barnsley
South Yorkshire
S70 2AS

Copyright © Craig Cabell, 2009

ISBN 978 1 84415 950 5

The right of Craig Cabell to be identified as author of
this Work has been asserted by him in accordance with
the Copyright, Designs and Patents Act 1988.

A CIP catalogue record for this book is available from the British Library.

All rights reserved. No part of this book may be reproduced or
transmitted in any form or by any means, electronic or mechanical
including photocopying, recording or by any information storage
and retrieval system, without permission from the Publisher in writing.

Printed and bound in England by
CPI UK

Pen & Sword Books Ltd incorporates the imprints of
Pen & Sword Aviation, Pen & Sword Maritime, Pen & Sword Military,
Wharncliffe Local History, Pen and Sword Select, Pen and Sword Military Classics,
Leo Cooper, Remember When, Seaforth Publishing and Frontline Publishing.

For a complete list of Pen & Sword titles please contact
PEN & SWORD BOOKS LIMITED
47 Church Street, Barnsley, South Yorkshire, S70 2AS, England
E-mail: enquiries@pen-and-sword.co.uk
Website: www.pen-and-sword.co.uk

While the author has taken all reasonable steps to track down and clear
copyright of images used, this has not proved possible in every case and
any unavoidable omission is regretted

Dedication

This book is dedicated to Charles Wheeler, Patrick Dalzel-Job, Lt Cdr D.M. Curtis, Captain Huntingdon-Whiteley, Captain Martin-Smith, Bill Thomas, James Powell and all the other men of 30 Assault Unit. My honour was to talk and meet with some of you – for you this modest tome, may your contribution never be forgotten.

Contents

Preface

'While he, Bond, had been playing Red Indians through the
years ... the real enemy had been working quietly, coldly,
without heroics, right there at his elbow.'

Casino Royale, Ian Fleming

Ian Fleming played an important role during the Second World
War as a Naval Intelligence officer. One of his many projects was
creating a crack team of commandos called 30 Assault Unit (30
AU) (formerly 30 Commando Unit). Their antics and derring-do
are one of the best-kept secrets of the Second World War.

Through archive material and interviews with surviving
veterans, the history of 30 AU is now pieced together to celebrate
the passion and bravery of one of the greatest commando units
of the Second World War.

30 AU's mission was to penetrate enemy lines, capture vital
intelligence and feed it back to London where it could be
assimilated and acted upon. They were the first unit ever to
attack a V-rocket establishment, and one of them, Patrick Dalzel-
Job, was reputably the main influence for Fleming's fictional
secret agent, James Bond. Other officers such as Lieutenant
Commander Curtis, Captain Huntingdon-Whiteley, Captain
Martin-Smith and Lieutenant McFee, remain unknown despite
significant bravery, until now.

On 4 July 2008, the BBC News at Ten announced the death of
Charles Wheeler. They spoke of his great contribution to

broadcasting, calling him the greatest broadcaster of all time. They showed an interview clip where he spoke of being brought up in Nazi Germany, how his friends – the Jews – used to hide in the woods. The one thing the BBC failed to speak of was Mr Wheeler's contribution to the Second World War, how he, as part of 30 AU, tenaciously interrogated prisoners of war and was at the sharp end throughout.

Charles Wheeler, Patrick Dalzel-Job and the other members of 30 AU are some of the true unsung heroes of the Second World War, as this book bares testament. Dalzel-Job was an important figure and Charles Wheeler was his brother-in-arms; but little is known of their bravery and tenacity.

This book highlights Charles Wheeler's contribution to the Second World War, which has been largely unappreciated until now. It is testament to the man's character that he never boasted about his contribution to 30 AU; but that is indicative of the war veteran of yesteryear. People like Charles Wheeler, Patrick Dalzel-Job and former broadcaster Raymond Baxter and, I dare say, many friends and relations of people who read this book, rarely spoke about their work during that period. For them, certain things were better off left unsaid, while nowadays, many ex-servicemen are keen to go into print regarding their days of action. Life now is more transparent in many ways. What we have in the following pages is the formation and implication of a very different type of commando unit, which contributed much to the success of the Allied forces during the Second World War and, because of their secret work, have been unappreciated for over sixty years.

Craig Cabell
London, 2009

Acknowledgements

The key people who made this book happen are: Charles Wheeler, Joan Bright Astley, Bill Thomas and James 'Bill' Powell. Their memories and perceptions became so very important when I applied the personal touch to the wealth of material found in archive; especially the bits that weren't mentioned. Each had a fascinating insight and important piece of the complex jigsaw that I was building, which was largely undocumented. Thank you for your memories and perceptions.

I would also like to thank good friends Steve White, Mark Ottowell, Dave Barlow and Graham A. Thomas, for their support during the early stages of this book. I would also like to thank my family for putting up with yet another writing project: Anita, Samantha, Nathan, Fern, my father Colin, Berny and Dave (all the people that have to endure my thought processes on an almost daily basis), and David Bowie and Bruce Springsteen for the companionship while I proofed the final manuscript. I would also like to thank Keith and Penny at The Marine public house, the spiritual home of 30 AU, and Diana, the secretary of 30 AU, who really helped in getting me on the road. It was an honour to talk to veterans of the unit – they really are so modest; to talk to the brilliant Charles Wheeler: 'What do you really know about us, Craig?' 'That's interesting, now read this and let's talk some more.' Bless you, dear sir, I hope I've done you justice.

I would like to thank Ted Poole for his kindness and generosity – the 30 AU print is a cherished possession and you are a great artist.

I would like to thank Steve Moore for that quirky advice that makes him so invaluable, a great, great friend and, last but by no means least, I would like to thank the men and women of the current Armed Forces who I have worked alongside for the past twenty years – it is your incredible professionalism, largely unappreciated in my opinion, that gave me the drive to write this book about some of your predecessors.

I would also like to thank Pen & Sword who put up with a late manuscript, my only excuse being I wanted to ensure that this book is as right as possible, which was a challenge because of the sensitivities surrounding the unit's work to this day; but we got there.

Sincerely, many thanks to all.

Craig Cabell
London, 2009

Notes on the Text

I would like to make it clear that I have split this history into two distinct parts for clarity. The first concerns the formation of the unit and its first year. During this period, the unit went through various tenuous titles, most commonly 30 Commando; but many other titles were used. For uniformity and ease for the reader, I call the unit 30 CU (30 Commando Unit) throughout. This may be technically incorrect for the purest; but then again, so are the various other titles, knick-names, misrepresentations, so 30 CU it is.

For the second part of this history I give the correct title of the unit as the newly formed 30 AU (30 Assault Unit); the title they were commonly referred to since the preparations of Operation OVERLORD started and a title that signified the end of their apprenticeship (and teething problems), forging them as the crack team of special commandos they were in Europe during the latter stages of the Second World War.

So, in short, the two parts don't just split 30 CU from 30 AU, they also split the fledgling unit from the professional one and give the reader a clear perception of each.

There are some disparate documents and books that concern 30 AU/Ian Fleming and, in order to provide a clear and unbiased basic history of the unit, I had to structure certain famous operations – such as OVERLORD – upon the basic facts and then add 30 AU into the mix. This simplistic but effective approach provided me with much quality background and clarity, but at the same time threw up several contradictions that were tricky to iron out. However, key books such as Alanbrooke's diaries, Montgomery's memoirs and Patton's diaries/memoirs proved to be most helpful, along with oddities such as the authorized biography of Cheshire and the modest autobiography of Patrick Dalzel-Job (see 'Further Reading' at the back of the book for full details).The main difficulties with the history of 30 AU came from the Top Secret work they did from Operation OVERLORD onwards. It is interesting that the official history misses out a lot of 30 AUs key moments and how they affected the broader canvas (what other units and the Allies were doing), which really is instrumental in ascertaining their huge importance to the final victory.

30 AU, no matter what way you look at it, played a major part in the plotting, capture and disablement of V1 and V2 rocket sites (under the respective titles Operation CROSSBOW and Operation BIG BEN). Furthermore, the veterans state that the importance of gathering intelligence concerning the V1s and V2s was paramount after OVERLORD and the chapters concerning this aspect of 30 AU's work have taken nine years to build. Primary research material has been hard but not impossible to gather, secondary research is rationalized at the endnotes or appendixes and is clearly marked as such. I labour the documenting of this area for the simple reason that it may assist any future researcher who stumbles across any additional primary documents worthy of capture in the future!

Although there is a tendency with works of this nature to use language and grammar evocative of the time – especially within certain quotes – I have refrained from doing so. Current word usage is used throughout, however many military abbreviations – and some more obscure ones – are used throughout the text to help the flow of the history. A key to these abbreviations follows this note. Also, the endnotes provide supporting descriptions and other information concerning units, departments, operations and perceptions from key personnel and are there to add greater clarity and perception to the modus operandi of 30 AU, without upsetting the flow or clarity of the text. So enjoy!

List of Abbreviations

30 AU	30 Assault Unit
30 CU	30 Commando Unit
ACOS (I)	Assistant Chief of Staff (Intelligence)
ANCXF	Headquarters Allied Expeditionary Naval Force
C-in-C	Commander-in-Chief
CCO	Chief of Combined Operations
Cdr	Commander
CO	Commanding Officer
Col	Colonel
COSD	Combined Operations Supply Department
DDOD (I)	Deputy Director Operations Division (Intelligence)
DNI	Director of Naval Intelligence
DNOR	Director of Naval Operations Requirements
DSR	Director of Supplier Relations
DTM (I)	Director of Torpedoes and Mines (Intelligence)
FSS	Field Security Section
HO	Home Office
HQ	Headquarters
ISLD	Inter-Service Liaison Department
ISRB	Inter-Service Research Bureau
JIC	Joint Intelligence Committee (US)
LCI	Landing Craft Intelligence
LCT	Landing Craft Tank
Lt	Lieutenant
Lt Cdr	Lieutenant Commander

ML	Motor Launch
MO 4/5	Medical Officer
MTB	Motor Torpedo Boat
MVSN	Milizia Volontaria per la Sicurezza Nazionale
NCO	Non Commissioned Officer
NID	Naval Intelligence Department
NOIC	Naval Officers in Charge
OR	Other Ranks
OSS	Office of Strategic Services
Pte	Private
PWB	Psychological Warfare Branch
RM	Royal Marines
RN	Royal Navy
RNVR	Royal Navy Voluntary Reserves
SACSEA	Supreme Allied Command South East Asia
SAS	Special Air Service
SEAC	South East Asia Command
SIS	Secret Intelligence Service
SOE	Secret Operations Executive
WT	Wireless/Transmitter

Introduction

'It was marvellous with what confidence and precision they went about their ordered world. Everything, you see, had been made to fit their needs.'

The Country of the Blind, H.G. Wells

There were many heroic episodes during the Second World War, many incidents that were over-analysed and documented by the multitude of veterans and biographers over the years. Some are instantly known to the public, even to those with little interest in military history, through impressive movies such as *The Battle of Britain* and *The Dam Busters*. But there are some very daring stories – begging for stardom – that have only recently come to light, such as the dive-bombing Spitfire missions (Operation BIG BEN) and the operational duties of 30 Assault Unit (30 AU), the latter a crack team of commandos formed by Commander Ian Fleming.

When I spoke to veterans in support of this book, which looks exclusively at the history of 30 AU, I was told of photographs in private hands that were banned from publication for 100 years because of the significance of their content. I was also told of wild stories, told to my interviewees by fellow veterans – now sadly departed – who believed they captured top Nazi scientists from the V rocket projects. These stories really didn't sit well with the history books (see Annex A). In short, the history of 30 AU is a complicated one and, even today, a highly political web.

One veteran said to me, 'You have an enormous job, because we didn't know at the time the detail of what we were doing, let alone our colleagues, and now some of them are not around to tell you.'

What I have decided to do with this modest work is provide a benchmark for future research, cross-checked, as far as possible, by the memories and perceptions of the people who were there. This is a process I went through before with Raymond Baxter and Operation BIG BEN – his input was invaluable to the accuracy of the book against the official squadron histories. He answered my questions, checked his own log book and read the final manuscript. He still had some concerns with reference to some obscure place names, which were amended in the paperback counterpart to that book, so the story is now an important document of what actually happened and has been used in reference for many other works regarding V2s – credited or not – and also made into a nice CGI film.

The fact is I'm not looking for plaudits here, the downside being that many reviewers and so-called 'experts' criticize new significant works, because they have been preaching a watered-down version of the facts for some time. When respected men such as Raymond Baxter offer their first-hand perception and memories, it shouldn't be questioned by the people who weren't there. Of course, memories fade and facts become blurred; but when presented with cold facts as laid down in archive, checked by veterans – or their perceptions added at least – it must be assumed that you are indeed on the right track when searching for the truth that hides in shadows.

It is indeed shocking that 30 AU haven't received the fame and, consequently, the praise they so richly deserve. Their antics are filled with such courage and derring-do it emanates the great fictional war movies of yesteryear, such as *The Guns of Navarone* and *Where Eagles Dare*.

30 AU were the real-life counterparts to those Second World War movies so loved by so many over the past sixty years. It is important to recognize as memory turns to history (i.e. as veterans of the Second World War pass away), the significance

and bravery of the people of that by-gone age, and pull together as many nuances of each individual story as possible. It is important that we do this for future generations to understand and appreciate the sacrifices of their forefathers. Also, it is important that we learn from the history books – in the best possible way – and cherish ingenuity alongside self-sacrifice. I for one am proud to have talked to so many great veterans of the Second World War, from family members to other unsung – and sung! – heroes in the interview room. I have worked significantly with each of the current Armed Forces within the modern civil service and I am filled with overwhelming respect for their stoicism and professionalism that has endured since time in memorial, despite unfair criticism and the break-up of regiments to appease politicians and people who don't know better.

Field Marshal Montgomery so perceptively stated in his memoirs that generation after generation of British people since the Second World War have had an easier life, so much so, it is now easy to pass off or ignore the courage that pushed this country towards the peace and prosperity we enjoy today. I couldn't agree more and that is why we need military publishers: to remind us of that courage.

So now let us learn what we can about 30 Assault Unit: their objectives, their work, who they were and their passions and frustrations. These men really existed and I extend my warmest thanks and respect to their memory – this book is homage to your work and achievements, gentlemen, I hope one day somebody gives you the credit you so richly deserve.

Part 1

30 Commando Unit

'A blunt instrument wielded by a Government department.'

Ian Fleming – describing his creation James Bond

Chapter 1

A Good Idea Borrowed

'Skorzeny turned all his saboteurs and terrorists into *SS Jagdverbande* for use behind enemy lines. Each Jagdverbande was divided into *Streifkorps* and then into *Kommandos*.'

Moonraker, Ian Fleming

When Ian Fleming wrote the original proposal for a 'Naval Intelligence Commando Unit' on 20 March 1942 as a 'Most Secret' paper[1] to his boss Rear Admiral John Godfrey, he credited in the first paragraph the influence of his idea: Obersturmbannfuehrer Otto Skorzeny and the German intelligence commandos. One specific raid influenced Fleming: that of the capture of Crete. In May 1941, Crete was lost to the German forces due to careful strategy instigated by Otto Skorzeny. Navy Intelligence officers learnt that Skorzeny had a specific role in the capture of the island, and how he gathered as much secret material from British headquarters in Maleme and Heraklion beforehand to find the British weaknesses and take the island. Skorzeny and his troops were completely successful. This impressed Fleming because he knew the British had to find something to counter such a smash-and-grab group of soldiers. But it wasn't just the German commandos that inspired Fleming to write his memo, there was something else.

During a trip to New York in 1941, Fleming and Godfrey[2] met with two highly influential people who introduced him to the nuances of special agent training. They were William Donovan and William Stephenson. They took him to Canada where he was shown the art of lock picking, safe blowing, underwater swimming and many other things that his future 'Red Indians' (the pet name Fleming gave his commando unit) would become experts in. So two disparate things came together at roughly the same time to create the germ of the idea of 30 Assault Unit (or 30 Commando as they were originally called).

Fleming's memo – the earliest official record of the birth of the unit – is quite succinct. It stated that the commandos would accompany the front line attack on any 'port or naval installation' and then capture intelligence before it could be 'destroyed by the defenders'.

The wording of the document is quite significant. It stated that as soon as all the intelligence had been acquired and fed back to London, 30 AU would attach itself to the front line and therefore place itself in a perfect position to drill into enemy territory (as a small, self-contained unit aside from the front line). Also, and quite importantly, 30 AU were there specifically for DNIs use. The information sought was that deemed of most interest to the Naval Intelligence Department (NID) – Fleming and Godfrey would later instigate a handbook outlining the specifics of what they should and shouldn't capture.

So the idea for 30 AU was 'borrowed' from the Nazis – but at the same time built upon – by Commander Ian Fleming of NID through his boss John Godfrey, who was more than determined to see his department reap the reward for the idea. We know this because in the original document outlining the new unit, Godfrey scribbled out Fleming's line to 'submit' the idea of 30 AU to CCO for further action, and wrote on the document that the unit would be developed 'in collaboration' with CCO. This is an important point because Godfrey saw the significance of the unit and wanted to keep the glory for himself and his department. Fleming's original memo is also important because he has been criticized for only coming up with laughable ideas during the Second World War. This book bares testament to his greatest idea, which was not just highly thought of, but made a major contribution to the war effort.

It is interesting how the idea for 30 AU came about. It fits a writer's creative style succinctly. Most writers admit that ideas for books don't come together from one source – two or three disparate things come together to form an interesting concept, and that's exactly what happened to Ian Fleming when creating 30 AU. His ability to think laterally created one of the greatest teams of commandos ever: 30 Assault Unit – Ian Fleming's Red Indians. But in the real world there has to be more than just a great idea, there have to be people who are prepared to understand and make that idea work. 30 AU would become an incredibly tactile unit; but it wasn't to begin with. There were many frustrations and lessons to be learnt. It was not all plain sailing and glory, and that must be distinctly understood. In fact, they upset many people on a huge learning curve where many lives were lost.

'Let us hope that these islands may, ere long, be made free and independent. Freedom and independence will bring with them industry and prosperity; and wherever these are found, arts and letters will flourish, and the improvement of the human race proceed.'

Southey's *Life of Nelson*

Chapter 2

Operational Duties

'Three principles will have an important bearing on any
operations designed to seize and exploit documents,
equipment and personnel required for intelligence purposes.'

Intelligence Assault Force Operations, August 1944

The operational duties of 30 Assault Unit were formally laid
down in August 1944 by the Office of Assistant Chief of Staff
(Supreme Headquarters Allied Expeditionary Force), for
posterity. Members of 30 AU had a small notebook that made
their basic operational duties clear from their inception. Before
we learn the history of the unit, let us first understand broadly
what their remit was: to capture and assimilate important
documents and equipment behind enemy lines that would help
London – specifically NID – in the war effort.

To do this, when deployed, 30 AU had to first understand the
target area and coordinate their assault. The element of surprise
was fundamental to their success because they had to arrest their
booty before it was destroyed by the enemy (any military
establishment would destroy their most important documents if
being taken over by the enemy seemed inevitable; so the element
of surprise was essential to 30 AU).

Once an establishment had been taken, the next exercise was
to provide safe storage and passage for the
documents/equipment back to London. Sometimes this was not
possible. When, shortly after D-Day, 30 AU entered a deserted

V1 rocket site, they had to go back through the lines and arrange the safe passage of Allied scientists, who were to visit the site later that day and professionally analyse it.

In short, 30 AU were aggressive intelligence gatherers. They would take the information – by force if necessary – from the enemy, behind enemy lines, and feed it back to HQ; but how did they organize themselves to be efficient in this type of exercise?

The task outlined for 30 AU was not in any way similar to that undertaken by ordinary combat troops. Their three performance indicators were:

1. The Capture of Buildings, Equipment and Personnel. These exercises would be carried out by combat troops with specialist assistance. The specialists would not be designated as anything other than ordinary soldiers as they would be of immense use to the enemy if captured. Specialists would be shielded from the main assault of the unit until the enemy was overcome, then they would be brought in. Sometimes, it wasn't necessary or practicable to use combat troops, so parachutists (in the widest meaning of the word) or underground resistance units could be used.[1]

2. The Assimilation of Intelligence Gathered. This was to be done in one of two ways: either on the spot (or at a nearby establishment best suited for such work), or have the equipment taken away and flown/sailed back to England (specifically Portsmouth). Sometimes the assimilation of intelligence would mean the interrogation of individuals. This would be undertaken by specialists, such as the aforementioned Charles Wheeler. There could be some considerable time between the taking of an establishment and the assimilation of intelligence, especially if the specialists needed were nowhere near the target area (for their own safety). 30 AU had to penetrate enemy lines, recce the site first and ensure the safe passage of the scientists they had to bring in to assimilate the intelligence at hand. Once all this had happened, 30 AU had to 'clear up', either evacuate important items, destroy them, or wait till they could hand over the

establishment to the 'occupational authorities' (more often than not the Americans).

3. A Composite Assault. This was a complex infiltration of troops that would set up a Forces Headquarters, fully supported by intelligence staff, combat troops (reinforced by appropriate service and specialist troops such as engineers, signals) and, depending on the factors set out for the operation, a number of specialist field teams. These were highly dangerous duties and would only be executed when a major target was sourced.

Underpinning these indicators were details of how to execute them. For example, setting up a Force Headquarters for 30 AU activity was a complex business. It would include two structured departments: Organisation and Responsibilities, the latter being split into four distinct areas: Personnel, Intelligence, Operations and Administration.

The organization of a Force Headquarters took the normal military lines for such a task, but with the addition of specific intelligence staff – and other specialists – needed for the intricacies of the operation. Because of this, a 'superior headquarters' (English or American) would have the task of choosing the targets for attack (this would ensure that the right specialists were selected for the right jobs and that the units work didn't impinge upon any other major operation being planned or executed).

Finally, there was the reserve force. This group would have sufficient technical and service personnel to ensure the smooth running of the headquarters throughout the operational duties i.e. when everyone else had vacated base.

The framework of 30 AU was very clear; but what about the individual's duties within it?

I have identified an Intelligence Officer, Charles Wheeler, who would become a 'tenacious interrogator', according to certain veterans I interviewed in my research for this book. As Wheeler is a known BBC personality, let us look at what his duties as a member of the 30 AU Intelligence staff would have been: apart from the fundamental tasks of any Intelligence Officer (collecting and distributing evaluated combat intelligence). Wheeler would have to carry out the following specialist tasks:

1. Distribute special information to specialist field teams, both before and during the operation.
2. Record the location and destination of documents, equipment and personnel.
3. Implement the policy of the physical handling of documents, equipment and the handling of individuals dangerous to the security of the unit or the larger remit of British/Allied security.
4. Interrogation and interviewing of 'friendly' persons or suspects.
5. Advice regarding the handling of special intelligence matters (as they arise).

It was made clear that the dissemination of intelligence gained should be confined to the Intelligence staff, as they evaluated it in the first place. The exception to this rule was any specialist information that fell outside the ability of the Intelligence Officer. In these cases the responsibility was escalated to the appropriate level, maybe the 'superior headquarters', or simply one of the specialists scientists. The Intelligence Officer had access to the scientists at all times, especially when writing any reports deemed necessary for a given operation.

All reports generated had to be distributed through existing army channels, as that was deemed the safest route to reach their target audience.

Language speakers – such as Wheeler – would also interrogate, interview and screen people, and physically translate and disseminate any recorded information.[2]

It is not practicable in this book to identify the job description or detail of every aspect of 30 AU, but to paint a broad picture of their skills and capabilities before detailing their history. That said, it should be understood what an important intelligence document looked like (at any given captured site), and who made the decision as to that document's importance and final destiny.

On arrival at the target area, specialist field teams made a rapid search of the establishment to ascertain if there was important documentation. This was the primary concern of the unit and field teams were not permitted to look only for information that they were interested in, but what every other field team associated with 30 AU was interested in.[3] So once the establishment was taken there could be a delay while the field teams were brought in. It was the job of the forward troops to keep control of the establishment while this work was carried out.

Once documents were found, they had to be transported safely back to HQ as soon as possible. Once this had been done, a very brief inventory of the contents of the site had to be written up by the specialist field team. It would only describe the general situation regarding documents, for example what general subjects were available for examination and what the general state of the target was. The inventory was expected to be no more than fifteen to twenty lines in length.

It should be mentioned here that permission had to be acquired from HQ for any piece of equipment to be removed from a target area for further investigation, because it would ultimately mean crating and shipping that equipment home, which shouldn't be necessary.[4]

30 AU were commandos and intelligence gatherers, not glorified rag-and-bone men who collected any old bric-a-brac, thus slowing them down or hindering them from executing the work they had to do. The difficulty of executing this high level of professionalism was described by Patrick Dalzel-Job quite eloquently in his autobiography *Arctic Snow to Dust of Normandy*:[5]

Unlike normal troops, our whole object was of course to get into our targets by slipping past the enemy's defences, and this was for the most part surprisingly easy. On the other hand, I have often thought how much was demanded of ... [my men], who sat or stood beside me in the open jeep as we drove slowly and watchfully along ominously silent roads ... it cannot have been at all the same thing for men who could only stare ahead, hands on steering wheel or finger on trigger, waiting for the next order and expecting at any moment to face the harsh rattle of a machine gun or the devastating burst of a road mine. Often, these tense conditions would last for many miles and hours.

The remit of 30 AU seems so cold and logical on paper, but what they did was not the 'norm' in the British Armed Forces during the Second World War and tensions would quickly become clear.

Chapter 3

The Unit is Formed

'Man in this troubled time,
Dark ocean,
Must act like Prometheus
And like Adam

... The people must tear free
From the harsh decree.'

Ibo, Victor Hugo

Due to Ian Fleming's memo, JIC accepted the idea of an intelligence unit (based upon Skorzeny's German commando unit) to participate in commando raids and to accompany the early assault waves in large-scale operations, in order to seize the high-grade enemy intelligence material before it could be destroyed.

The unit was formed from the Special Service Brigade and called 30 Commando (30 CU).[1] It was then split into three sections: Royal Navy, Royal Marines and Army. The unit was then – after much delay and deliberation, i.e. Godfrey's protests – placed under the Chief of Combined Operations (CCO).

Once formed, the unit was temporarily placed under the command of Commander Red Ryder VC RN, a member of CCOs naval training staff. Major W.G. Cass, The Buffs, a regular officer with intelligence experience who was appointed second in command, while Commander Ian Fleming represented Director of Naval Intelligence's (DNIs) interests, which must have been Godfrey's final compromise (to keep DNI involvement).

In November 1942, a war establishment was given to the unit, under the cover name of the Special Engineering Unit of the Special Service Brigade. An office for the planning staff was designated in COHQ and an independent headquarters was awarded at Amersham, where the troops were billeted in private houses.

The original organization was:

Commanding Officer: Commander Ryder VC RN
Second in Command: Major Cass, The Buffs

No. 36 RN Troop: 1 x Lieutenant Commander RNVR, 3 x Lieutenants 'RNVR, 3 x Sub Lieutenants RNVR
No. 33 RM Troop: 2 x Captains RM, 20 x other ranks RM
No. 34 Army Troop: 2 x Captains (later increased to 4), 12 other ranks.

On the face of it the Royal Navy didn't fair too well, especially when it was them who devised the unit in the first place! Indeed, the internal squabbles about the chain of command within the unit and its commanding body was something changed many times during the unit's life and only really sorted after D-Day.

The RN Troop was manned by RNVR officers chosen from volunteers for hazardous service. Most of these originally selected lacked the qualifications and aptitude required for the type of work envisaged for the unit. Only three of them, Lieutenant Commander Q.T.P. Riley RNVR, Lieutenant D.M.C. Curtis DSC RNVR and Sub Lieutenant G. McFee RNVR remained with the unit for any length of time and ostensibly played any part in the operational duties of the unit.

Let us briefly look at who these men were in order to get a better snapshot of the type of person designated 30 CU calibre in its formative stages.

Lieutenant Commander Riley was a graduate of Cambridge University. Between 1930 and 1937 he was engaged continuously on polar exploration, taking part in two expeditions, one to Greenland and one to the Antarctic. He joined the RNVR in 1939 but was transferred temporarily to a special battalion of the Scots Guards, which had been mobilized to operate in Finland. This campaign did not materialize, however, and Lieutenant Commander Riley returned to RNVR serving on the staff of Brigadier Gubbins in Norway where he was Mentioned in Despatches. On his return he was appointed to Combined Operations as a Flotilla Officer and eventually served in Iceland as instructor in winter warfare. On his recovery from injuries received in this service, he was selected by Commander Ryder for 30 CU.

Lieutenant Curtis graduated at Oxford and completed his studies on the Continent. He became a solicitor in 1935, joined the RNVSR in 1936 and was called up to RNVR in February 1940. He served at first in Coastal Forces and took part in the raids of St Nazaire and Dieppe. For his part in the former he received the immediate award of the DSC. Subsequently he was engaged in special operations in home waters and joined 30 CU on its formation. Lieutenant Curtis was fluent in French and German.

Sub Lieutenant McFee was an Incorporated Accountant and at the outbreak of war held a position in the Accounts Department of the City Treasurer of Dundee. He joined the RNVR and on receiving his commission volunteered for hazardous service. As a consequence he was appointed to 30 CU.

The RM Troops were volunteers for commando service and were chosen by Captain H.O. Huntingdon-Whiteley RM, the troop leader, and Captain J.S. Hargreaves-Heap RM, the administration officer. Huntingdon-Whiteley was a regular marine officer who had been serving with 40 RM Commando before being appointed to 30 CU. He was a fine athlete and musician. Hargeaves-Heap was studying to be an actuary before joining the Royal Marines, having previously lived for a time in Vienna. He was fluent in French and German. He joined 30 CU after having taken part in the raid on Dieppe.

The selection of the other ranks was not in all cases satisfactory, probably on account of the immaturity of the officers responsible for it. This caused major problems with discipline within the RM sector of the unit, bringing the whole of 30 CU into disrepute!

The Army Troop favoured better and were selected by Major Cass from existing commando units and were specifically selected for their skills in particular tasks. Approximately one third of them were ex-policemen, while the rest came from other walks of life as diverse as chemists, draughtsmen and mechanics. Their discipline, bearing and physique were exceptional.

The Army Troop leader was Captain J.A. Ward, a regular officer in the British Army. Ward had seen service in France 1939/40 and had been part of commando raids on Vaagso and Lofoten in 3 Commando. The Administrative Officer was Captain T. Belcher, South Staffs Regiment, who joined the unit from 12 Commando. The other officers selected were Captain T. Hill, General List, a French linguist, and Lieutenant S. Tucker, Intelligence Corps, who had served in the Special Branch of Scotland Yard.

So now we know a little about some of the officers, let's look at their training scheme and understand the nuances of that. The unit as a whole received the following programme of basic training:

1. Assault and street fighting course on the usual commando lines.
2. The handling of small arms, mortars and hand grenades.
3. Enemy mines and booby traps.
4. The handling of explosives, demolitions and counter-demolitions.
5. The recognition of enemy uniforms, badges, weapons and vehicles.

In addition, the RN and Army Troops, together with a few of the Royal Marines, were instructed in:

1. Parachute jumping.
2. The handling of small boats.
3. The recognition of enemy documents.
4. The searching of premises and recovery of material from salvage, safe breaking and lock picking.
5. The searching of persons and the care of prisoners of war.
6. The recognition of individuals from photographs and descriptions.
7. Escaping drill, instruction for activities as prisoners of war and conduct under interrogation.

The RN and Army Troops also took an intensive course in the photography of equipment and documents.

The officers of the RN Troop, who were regarded as specialists in the intelligence aspects of the unit's activities, were divided into groups to take courses in enemy sea mines, torpedoes, electronics, hydrophones and asdic gear, the internal layout of submarines, the organization of enemy Armed Forces and Intelligence services, and also languages (primarily German and Italian). Certain officers also qualified as divers.

The basic training programme was comprehensive and well suited to the requirements of individual operations. It suffered from the serious disadvantage of not being applied uniformly to the entire unit. The training of the RM Troop in particular was neglected, probably due to the discipline problems they endured and these deficiencies were later reflected in operations. The Army Troop by comparison shone out.

When I spoke to 30 AU veterans in February 2008, they told me that they volunteered for any additional training that came their way from hazardous training to diving, mainly because the successful execution of such training gave them more money, indeed some of the subalterns were earning more than some of the officers as a consequence!

The administration of the RN Troop did cause some problems. In November 1942, naval personnel, apart from chaplains and surgeons attached to the RM commandos, could not be put into SS Brigade. There was no procedure for doing so. Since approval could not be obtained for the unit to be commissioned as a ship or administered by the Admiralty through DNI or DDOD (I), officers of the RN Troop were eventually appointed to HMS President for duty outside the Admiralty with CCO (Special Engineering Unit). RM and Army personnel were appointed to SS Brigade without any problems. This red tape concerning the RN Troop was a portent of future problems with this quirky new unit.

Each troop was independently responsible for its own supplies.

No war establishment could be allotted to the RN Troop since there was no procedure upon which it could be based, and COHQ, the only authority to which RN Troop could look for equipment, was not a supply organization. Eventually the RN Troop was obliged to draw its stores and equipment from such sources as were available, including the Combined Operations Supply Depot (COSD), West Meon, the Special Brigade, and RN stores.

The RM and Army Troops were accorded basic war establishments, proportionate to their numbers, on the same scale as normal commando units, expanded by the special equipment needed by the nature of their operations. These stores were drawn originally from SS Brigade.

There was much groundwork employed in the setting up of 30 CU, mainly because such a diverse unit had never been formed before. Indeed, throughout their life they encountered many problems. They were the mavericks that didn't do things by the book. The officers had to think on their feet a little more than their 'regular' counterparts and, also, there was the heartache of knowing that much of what they were doing had the caveat 'Secret' or above. From the beginning to the end of their life, 30 CU had much stacked up against them.

Chapter 4

Let's See Action

'Clarity of thought is essential. I am a great believer in live and let live, but not at the expense of my British way of life.'

Soldier – the Autobiography, General Sir Mike Jackson

It is clear that the structure of 30 CU took a lot of working out. They had broken the mode of tradition and there were frustrations about this, but the war couldn't wait, it was taking lives every day. In short, 30 CU had to be activated, ready or not.

While High Command argued about the nuances of the make-up of the unit, Godfrey called Huntingdon-Whiteley in with members of 40 RM. Ian Fleming sat in and listened to the brief: to attempt the capture of a certain German headquarters in Dieppe.

This was the first opportunity for members of the unit to prove themselves. On 12 August 1942, Huntingdon-Whitely and some men from 40 RM Commando sailed out to the shore of Dieppe. Unfortunately, they were spotted and sunk, with the frustration of spending several hours in the water before being picked up!

Godfrey and Fleming must have been pretty embarrassed by this and questioned the validity of the unit – were they asking them to do the impossible? Perhaps it was just 'jolly bad luck', perhaps the success of such a unit had to be based upon some well-earned good luck? But if Skorzeny got away with it, why couldn't they? They would try again, but the next time they would have cover from troops in a much larger operation. They needed the opportunity to sneak in and sneak out again, while the enemy was engaged on other matters.

On 8 November 1942, 30 CU took part in Operation TORCH (the Allied landings in North Africa). Deception plans had been laid down by the Joint Planning Staff (namely John Bevan and Dennis Wheatley) under the code name 'Solo One'. This attempted to focus the enemy on Norway rather than Africa,[1] but it became clear that once TORCH convoys sailed, U-boats or long-range enemy aircraft would see them heading west rather than north and know that they had been deceived. So Bevan and Wheatley changed the deception location to the Azores and then, once at the Straits of Gibraltar, Sardinia, followed by Sicily then Greece.[2]

30 CU's mission, as part of the US side of the operation, was pretty clear: capture material from the French Naval Headquarters at Algiers.

Lieutenant Curtis headed 33 Section and became part of 'King Terminal', a platoon of 600 US troops whose job it was to seize the dockyard as well as the headquarters at Algiers.

Although 33 Section had the benefit of being part of a larger platoon, they were still left to their own devices once they reached the dockyard. The Americans had their work cut out taking the southern end only and couldn't even give 33 Section a smattering of men to help them take the French Naval Headquarters.

Curtis wasn't happy and suggested that 33 Section be released to merge with 6 Commando and land on a beach 4 miles to the north-west of the town, and was likely to get to the French Naval Headquarters before 'King Terminal'. His suggestion was turned down as the 7,000 men taking part in that raid had already been deployed!

A second failure was now facing 30 CU and things seemed to be going from bad to worse when HMS *Malcolm*, in which 33 Section were being carried, came under attack. The ship was soon disabled and set alight by a direct hit in the boiler room.

Curtis and his men threw as much ammunition overboard as

possible but soon had to evacuate themselves, reporting aboard HMS *Bulolo*. His duty clear, Curtis sought permission to land 33 Section at Sidi Ferruch, so they could join with 168 US Regimental Combat Team for the final assault on the city, which was due to take place early the next morning. Permission was granted and 33 Section landed at 1535hrs on 8 November and immediately moved off towards Algiers by way of Cheragas, and El Bihar.

Things seemed to be finally working out for Curtis and his men, but it was soon learnt that an armistice had been declared at 0900hrs. This meant that a search of the French Naval Headquarters was now out of the question. Out of determination and just a little frustration, Curtis decided to take the headquarters of the Italian Armistice Commission in the Villa El Djenna at St Rapael, about a mile south-east of El Bihar.

33 Section arrived at 0930hrs and seven prisoners were taken. These were given to the French under the terms of the Armistice. Although no documents of any importance were discovered, a WT transmitter was taken intact and its settings noted. The premises were handed over at 1130hrs, thus making short successful work for 33 Section.

10 November was spent arranging the release of Allied prisoners, mostly US troops taken during the assault on the dockyard, who were being held by the French Navy. On 11 November, 33 Section took part in a search of Hotel Aletti, where the German Armistice Commission had been quartered. Again, no documents were found.

On 12 November, Curtis heard that some German members of the Armistice Commission had been captured near Sidi Ferruch. They had been attempting to escape in a car at the time. Some interesting 'papers' had been found on them. Curtis made many inquiries regarding these papers and eventually found that they had been acquired by the office of the US Army Intelligence.

Curtis couldn't have been too happy with his work. He had been compromised severely, first by the enemy on the dockside but then by the American forces and their own self-importance.

33 Section sailed to Gibraltar on 15 November and arrived on

the 20th. Curtis reported to Lieutenant Commander Bacon. After a reasonable discussion it was decided that Curtis should return to Algiers with two RMs in order to conduct a meticulous search of all enemy headquarters in the area. There was every reason to believe that US troops would have overlooked as boring an issue as enemy documentation, so this was an opportunity for Curtis to show his mettle.

This task was completed on 3 December when Curtis returned to London with a lot of useful information. The Admiralty wrote of the antics of Curtis and 33 Section, 'This operation may be regarded as successful, since, although the original main objective was not taken, valuable material was recovered from a target of opportunity.'

It was known that a commando unit's work was difficult at best and for Curtis to return with something of significance was a major step in the right direction, or so NID would have everyone believe.

But what about the failure of taking the French Naval Headquarters? Who was really to blame for that? It was summarized that intelligence relating to the defence of Algiers harbour was incomplete, that the official forecast of non-resistance on the part of the French Navy and coastal defences was over-optimistic and the use of 600 US men in the capture of the headquarters was inadequate. In fact, the US troops who landed from HMS *Brook* were quickly overcome and taken prisoner, so in short the Americans, not the British, were to blame.

It was subsequently discovered that the headquarters 33 Section was ordered to take was guarded by approximately 2,000 men and numerous machine-gun posts.

In hindsight, 33 Section were quite fortunate as intelligence had been poor and they would have almost certainly been lost if they had got anywhere near the headquarters. This was fully recognized by DNI and Fleming, who praised Curtis most highly and his ability to adapt, overcome and salvage something from a poorly planned operation. Indeed their praise was vindicated when all the captured material had made its way back to London via Lieutenant Commander Bacon. By ingenuity rather than default, 30 CU had chalked up their first success. Begrudgingly it was confirmed that through Operation TORCH 30 CU had their uses. It was also recognized that 33 Section had reached the headquarters of the Italian Armistice Commission two clear hours ahead of anyone else.

Lieutenant Curtis was mentioned in despatches.

'The Soldier must at all times be physically and mentally fit to answer the calls on the Army in many parts of the world; and he cannot be mentally fit unless he is first physically fit.'

From the Foreword to the *Army Physical Training Corps Centenary 1860-1960*, Field Marshal The Viscount Montgomery of Alamein

Chapter 5

Deeper into Africa

'Forward to Tunis! Drive the enemy into the sea!'

Message to the Army from General Montgomery

Godfrey and Fleming were keen to build upon the TORCH success, believing that there was still much information in North Africa to capture and learn from, or as they put it, '[to learn from] the liquidation of enemy forces in North Africa'. A stronger team from 30 CU was deemed necessary to achieve this, consisting of the newly promoted Curtis, Captain Huntingdon-Whitely and Lieutenant McFee, with seventeen Royal Marines and an RN Writer. They sailed to the Mediterranean in February 1943 and were placed under the command of C-in-C Mediterranean for operations against Naval Intelligence targets in Tunisia.

It is here that 30 CU began to forge its independence. They were given their own staff car, stores and three jeeps. It is no secret that Commander Ian Fleming arranged such things for them. Not only is this documented thoroughly in the National Archive,[1] it was explained to me by veterans of 30 AU who attributed their 'excellent facilities' to their benefactor and unsung hero Ian Fleming, who they never met but they knew he was behind them all the way.[2]

A joint headquarters was set up at Bone with the Mediterranean section of DDOD (I)'s force, and while the section was waiting for favourable weather, it took part in special boat and parachute training with 62 Commando, later known as the SAS Regiment.

Work soon got underway after this. Towards the end of March, Curtis, Huntingdon-Whiteley and ten RMs set out in their three jeeps, accompanied by two motorbikes, to pass from the Eighteenth Army Group Headquarters near Al Beida in the First Army Area, to Monty's Eighth Army, south of Gabes. However, on the nights of 5 and 6 April 1943, a small raid was made against Galita Island. The forces taking part comprised two sections of 62 Commando and a section of 30 CU under Lieutenant McFee. The operation was aborted when a strong line of defence was discovered.

Meanwhile the rest of 30 CU were embroiled with Monty's Eighth Army and, because they were such a powerful force, 30 CU's work with them can only be considered as 'exercise', they didn't carry out uniform duties with the Eighth, they did their own job.

Curtis reported to the Intelligence staff of the Eighth Army on arrival where he was warmly welcomed. Arrangements were made for 33 Troop of 30 CU to be accommodated with the leading troops for the advance westwards from Gabes.

The battle opened over two nights (6/7 and 7/8 April), Curtis and his section moved up and joined the forward headquarters of the 51st (Highland) Division, who gave the party permission to operate with the assault troops.

At 0930hrs on 8 April, the lighthouse and coast defence batteries at La Skirra were captured and searched by 33 Troop. Two Italian prisoners were taken but no intelligence material of any importance was discovered.

On 9 April, they entered Mahares with the leading troops. During an engagement with enemy tanks Curtis was slightly wounded. However, early on 10 April, the lighthouse and batteries at Thina were taken. After the premises had been searched the party carried on with the leading troops of the Highland Division and entered the town of Sfax, where it was divided into two sections, one to handle the headquarters of the Italian Navy, the other that of the Germany Army. Later a search was made of the building occupied by the Italian Army. Documents discovered were mainly about local naval interest but still handed to the relevant Intelligence people.

At approximately 0300hrs on the morning of 12 April, 33 Troop moved towards Sousse and entered the town while the New Zealand faction of the Division was still fighting around Kalaa-Srira. The troop was divided, one section being detailed to deal with the German headquarters in Sousse itself, the other being sent to an Italian Naval section some 10 miles out in the middle of nowhere on the road to Monastir.

Curtis proceeded to Sousse harbour in order to examine some damaged vessels that were lying there, including two German LCTs. Photographs were taken of the latter. At the request of the Eighth Army, Curtis carried out an inspection of the harbour with a view to the possibility of its immediate use by LCTs. He reported that apart from the possibility of the entrance being closed with sea mines, he considered that LCTs could enter and unload at once.

The Troop left Sousse on 13 April and travelled back to Bone, arriving on the 14th and handing over their findings to SOI Algiers (the most important elements captured were annotated charts taken from the Italian Naval headquarters at Sfax).

The overall exercise assisted 30 CU to develop its fieldcraft for their particular assaults: gaining the maximum surprise and minimum amount of casualties. So far, Curtis was the only man who had received a wound.

When Eighth Army reached Enfidaville, Curtis and his Troop returned to the First Army front. Once there it was learnt that 30 CU had been drafted to a temporary organization called S Force. This had been formed by Lieutenant Colonel Strangeways to handle intelligence targets in Tunis and Bizerta. Many interested parties played a role in S Force: FSS, SIS, SOE, SIB, PWB and Civil Affairs and three squadrons of the RAF.

S Force were not designed to take the intelligence themselves, unlike 30 CU, so a request was made for 33 Troop (30 CU) – or at least one faction from within it – to accompany the leading Troop in their assault on Tunis. This was granted on the proviso that anything captured was produced for inspection for Officer Commanding before being shipped to C-in-C Mediterranean.

Tunis and Bizerta fell simultaneously and, since it was expected that the Afrika Korps would fight to the last man, Curtis did not consider it prudent to divide his small force and decided to concentrate on Tunis (this and the fact that he recognized that extensive demolition had occurred in Bizerta that would have made the capture of important material difficult anyway).

All this may seem relatively easy work but when one considers that 33 Troop left S Force camp, Testor, at 1630hrs on 7 May and was still moving on towards a second objective (after the Navy bases at Tunis) at 0545hrs on 8 May, a clear example of the dedication and endurance of 30 CU is appreciated.

S Force couldn't get to Tunis by road until 8 May where they were met by 33 Troop. Together they pushed forwards and the operational headquarters of the airfield at El Aouina was captured after 'a short skirmish'. Some valuable materiel was acquired, although the enemy had time to destroy most of it. That said, more material was gathered from other less hostile Headquarters.

Captain Huntingdon-Whiteley and half the Troop went onto Bizerta on 9 May, leaving the rest to clear up targets in the Tunis area.

All captured material of immediate importance was transported to Algiers by air on 11 and 13 May.

Curtis was slightly critical about S Force, as it had many non-combatant personnel attached to it, and said that he could have reached its targets in Tunis a whole twenty-four hours earlier if he didn't have the extra baggage; he was much more content – and felt more professional – with the Eighth Army. That said, the material captured in Tunis was thought to be of 'considerable value' and the unit took 252 prisoners without suffering any casualties itself. This was considered a major success.

In June, a party of eight RMs under Huntingdon-Whiteley took part in the capture of Pantelleria. There was little of importance captured.

Although MI6 assisted 30 CU at Headquarters with codes and ciphers, these were not practical for operational use, simply because units could not be contacted.

The North Africa operations of 30 CU were overall not a fantastic success but they did provide some very interesting material. NID wasn't in constant touch, they had drawn up a wish list of items for capture and received some as a consequence, they then went on to write a document about 'How To Create an Intelligence Gathering Commando Unit', which, as it transpired, wasn't much use to anyone after 30 AU was disbanded after the war. That said, the lessons learned from the North Africa operations helped form the nucleus of 30 AU and its modus operandi. The main point being that more manpower was needed, which they received. Also, more equipment was needed and received, due to Ian Fleming.

Fleming felt that 30 CU had been taken away from their objective and purpose. It can also be said that other government departments, namely the SOE wanted a slice of 30 CU, which they got under S Force.

On a more positive note, after the conclusion of the North Africa campaign Lieutenant Commander Curtis was awarded a bar to his DSC and Captain Huntingdon-Whiteley and Sergeant J. Kruthoffer RM were mentioned in despatches. 30 CU had done enough to win some respect cutting their teeth in Africa.

Chapter 6

30 CU Undergoes a Reshuffle

'The immortal march of the Eighth Army from the gates of Cairo along the Africa shore through Tunisia, through Sicily, has now carried its ever-victorious soldiers and their world-honoured commander far into Italy towards the gates of Rome. The scene changes and vastly expands. A great task accomplished gives place to a greater in which the same unfailing spirit will win for all true men a full and glorious reward.'

Winston Churchill

30 CU had worked alongside Monty's glorious Eighth Army, yet they were not a radical or even strategic part of it. By Christmas, General Montgomery would leave Eighth Army, become part of the European strategy and, as a consequence, would cross paths with 30 CU again in a much more radical way.

At the start of the year, major changes would happen within 30 CU's chain of command. First Commander Ryder transferred to Force J. He was succeeded by Major Cass, Lieutenant Commander Riley taking on Cass's previous post (leader of 33 RN or Technical Troop). In April 1943, Major Cass left the unit to take up an appointment in South-East Asia and Lieutenant Commander Riley became Formation Commander.

This was all natural posting activity, but it wasn't the same within the RN Troop. Two officers were got rid of because they couldn't cut the mustard. Their replacements were Lieutenant C.W.H.J. Philips RNVR from MO4 Cairo and Sub Lieutenant

D.N. Davies RNVR from 14 Commando.

Philips was a qualified air pilot who had travelled widely before the war and had held a diplomatic appointment in Rome. He had also served with the SOE and could possibly have been known to Fleming as NID clearly had dealings with that department.

There were changes in the Army Troop too: Lieutenant Tucker had been badly injured in a parachute accident and another lieutenant was involved in an accident with a hand grenade. Their places were taken by Captain P. Martin-Smith (Worcestershire Regiment, 12 Commando). Martin-Smith was an all-round athlete and an exceptional linguist, being able to pass himself off as a Frenchman or German.

Lieutenant Philips soon volunteered for flying duties with the Fleet Air Arm. He was accepted on the basis that a substitute be found for him. This came in the form of Captain T.J. Glanville, General List, from the SIS. Glanville had a working knowledge of most European languages. Like Philips, Glanville had experience in the SOE. He had volunteered to work in 30 CU.

So a vivid picture of the growing 30 CU can be appreciated at this juncture:

No. 36 (Naval or Technical Troop)

1 Lieutenant Commander RNVR
3 Lieutenants RNVR
1Sub Lieutenant RNVR
1 PO Signalman
1 Writer

No. 33 RM Troop

2 officers
20 other ranks RM

No. 34 (Army Troop)

5 officers
2 other ranks

It was noticed that the RN and Army Troops were one under and one over establishment. This difficulty was addressed by arranging for Captain Glanville to 'relinquish' his Army commission and join the RNVR in which he was granted a probationary commission with the acting rank of Lieutenant! The training programmes for 30 CU at this time run thus:

RN Troop: partly trained at Amersham on general commando lines but with additional courses including intelligence work and language: Italian.

No. 33 RM Troop: commando assault and battle courses, with intense training on street fighting. One section qualified as parachute jumpers; but no intelligence work was undertaken. This may be due to the early behaviour problems experienced within the RM Troop.

No. 34 Army Troop: completed a full training package as detailed by Major Cass, which included the obligatory commando, language and intelligence packages.

Once the training was completed, Lieutenant Commander Riley flew to Algiers[1] where he made final arrangements for 30 CU's North Africa campaign. Once completed, the unit joined him on 17 June, although they sailed there in a HM transporter bound for Algiers!

It was on 29 June that the formation parade took place and the ongoing work of the unit became clear: Lieutenant Commander Riley, Lieutenant Davies and Captain Huntingdon-Whitely took command of 8 RM ORs to take part in an assault on the complex radar stations at Cape Passero, Sicily; Lieutenant McFee, Captain P. Martin-Smith and seven Army ORs were designated to land east of Cape Passero to back up the radar station assault team; Lieutenant Glanville and eight RM ORs were to follow McFee with transport and stores; Lieutenant Philips, Captain Belcher and nine Army ORs were to proceed to Alexandria in order to participate in operations in the eastern Mediterranean;

Lieutenant Commander Curtis, with one Naval Rating and three Royal Marine ORs were to remain in North Africa for special training in preparation for their part in Operation BANTAM (which was eventually aborted);[2] Lt Orton, Captain Hargreaves-Heap and the remainder of the RM ORs were to organize the transfer of the unit's headquarters from Bone to Sicily; Captain Ward and one Army OR were to establish contact with the local representatives of the various clandestine organizations with whom the unit was to collaborate.

It was now time for 30 CU to come of age. Radical training and chain of command had been put in place and some less able officers got rid of. 30 CU stepped up a gear and began to move things forwards.

Things had changed radically back in NID as well. Fleming's boss Godfrey had moved on from his post as DNI and was replaced by Commodore E.G.N. Rushbrooke. Fleming had enjoyed a great deal of freedom with Godfrey but didn't know if this would be extended to him by the new boss.

Fleming briefed Rushbrooke concerning 30 CU's work. He mentioned that they had captured a map of enemy minefields and defences at Sicily recently and that they were planning a specific operation that seemed, to the Commodore, to make sense.

For the record, Fleming had little to fear from the new boss, as Godfrey had left a glowing report on his Commander RNVR, the crux of it stating: '[Fleming] has conducted himself very greatly to my satisfaction. His zeal, ability, and judgement are altogether exceptional.'

So not only had 30 CU undergone a reshuffle of command, so had NID. Now it was time to get more immersed in the intricacies of commando intelligence gathering.

'This was going to be dirty work and Bond, because he belonged to the Double-O Section, had to be chosen for it.'

The Living Daylights, Ian Fleming

Chapter 7

Cape Passero and Other Difficulties

'Men trained and experienced ... as well as being trained to fight, ought to be regarded as skilled tradesmen, and paid as such. It is no excuse for not so treating them, there is no demand for their special skills outside the Armed Services.'

Arctic Snow to Dust of Normandy, Patrick Dalzel-Job

In the spring of 2007 I met with several veterans of 30 AU who told me that they volunteered for as much specialized training as possible because, if they passed it, they would be awarded extra pay for taking on that specialization. Within 30 CU there was much opportunity for extra skills, from safe blowing, specialized ballistics training, parachuting, sub-aqua/diving techniques and much more. So it was the lure of extra pay as well as professional pride/duty that fuelled the ORs to take on more training within the unit.

The training 30 CU/AU went through, plus the men involved, influenced Fleming in his writing of the James Bond novels ten years later, such was the tenacity and fitness of the men who formed the unit. Bond would undergo training in Scotland Yard, just as 30 CU did, and the fictitious M served on the same ship as John Godfrey, strongly suggesting him to be the real-life M counterpart.

The Allied invasion of Sicily started with airborne operations at

0245hrs on 10 July 1943. At 0500hrs landings were made from the sea and the two sections of 30 CU (as designated), began their assault, one on Cape Passero and the other on the Western beaches towards Pozzallo.

Lieutenant Commander Riley's main target was the long-range early warning installation, consisting of a Wassermann set with girder type aerial array. Surprisingly, this was easily taken as the occupants surrendered without a fight. Riley's team managed to capture important documentation, including operational log books.

At precisely the same time, Captain Huntington-Whitely and Lieutenant McFee's team captured WT equipment and relevant documents, and Lieutenant Davies and his team captured a mobile Telefunken VHF set with several interesting features.

Lieutenant Glanville had landed with his convoy at Porto Palo. This was not the designated area but Glanville was diverted due to possible U-boat activity. The convoy had to make its way cross-country to the rendezvous fixed for 0900hrs the following morning at Wassermann tower. However, on the way, a mobile coast-watcher radar set was found. The crew had all been killed and the set damaged by shellfire. Documents of very high importance were found, including a technical handbook on the Wurzburg (Telefunken) series of radar sets, operators' logs and, on the officer commanding, a notebook recording courses taken in radar operation.

After the fall of Pachino and Porto Palo there was an outbreak of looting by Sicilians. This led to some officers and ORs from 30 CU policing the area. A headquarters was set up in the lighthouse at Porto Palo, where all captured material was logged and crated. On 12 July, most of it was shipped to Malta for the Mediterranean Fleet to take home, under the watchful eye of Lieutenant Davies.

Additionally, Private Heath of the Army section took many photographs, which were of immense use to the authorities.

The operation was deemed to be successful but it was noted that some material of high importance was missed. This was due to too much time being spent on policing and repairing enemy vehicles. So, despite all the good 30 CU did, there were still 'Lessons to be Learnt'.

Back in London, Commander Fleming reported the success to his new boss, noting that 30 CU were still working hard in theatre. He desperately wanted 30 CU to be successful, his other glorious plans, such as Operation RUTHLESS, hadn't really taken off, so his reports to DNI were very 'glass half filled' rather than 'half empty'; time would vindicate his optimism.

On 12 July, Lieutenant McFee, Captain Martin-Smith and the Army Troop took part in the advance on Syracuse, which fell the same day. This was just an act of going through the motions, as the Troop was far too late to capture documents of any significance.

Not to be put off McFee and Martin-Smith's section carried on to the seaplane base near Augusta, where they arrived on 13 July. Valuable documents were captured there. From there they moved on and were the first unit into the town and port area, where they met with some enemy resistance. After searching the Italian Naval headquarters and port buildings, the section returned to Syracuse with important documentation.

This was not the end of this particular operation. Once the captured documents were analysed, it was felt that much more important material could have been captured and a second team of RMs, led by Captain Huntingdon-Whitely, would be released to make a detailed search of the whole area. The Italian-speaking Glanville also joined the section.

Although they were only gone a single day, the section had a very interesting time. The main headquarters of the Italian Navy was housed in a series of vaults protected by reinforced concrete. Most of the documentation had been burnt or flooded. Undeterred, 30 CU interrogated the Italian dockyard workers and found that the main arsenal had been transferred to the caves of Mellili, an extensive series of caverns, which had been excavated under the hills lying to the north of the main road from Syracuse to Augusta. They immediately set off to the location and discovered a long-range WT station and extensive Naval stores of ordnance and underwater weapons. However,

SOI Levant had discovered Mellili a few hours previously and had captured the Italian C-in-C and documentation relating to attacks on the Malta convoys. Glanville agreed to leave Mellili to Levant, who had a group of Italian document experts on hand. 30 CU returned to Augusta to find troops looting the town. Again, 30 CU found themselves policing the area until RM police moved in who looked upon Glanville's team with suspicion, not totally believing that 30 CU weren't looters themselves.

Glanville was eventually given permission to conduct his searches and, although he found much destroyed documentation, he did find equipment relating to anti-aircraft gunnery with relevant handbooks.

The ashes and charred paper from the underground rooms where secret work had been done were carefully sorted and any scrap of ash or paper that looked likely to hold valuable intelligence was packed between layers of glass wool in a light fibre suitcase for shipment to Malta. On 14 July, the captured material was sorted, crated and sent to COIS Med.

Again there were 'Lessons Learnt', for example, the absence of an Italian speaker early on meant 30 CU were not first on the scene at Mellili, where their thunder was seriously stolen. Also, inadequate resources in men, fire-fighting equipment and communications resulted in some tough criticism too.

It is clear that 30 CU were a dedicated and professional body of men during these early stages with regard to the way they went about their business, but when asked to take part in the bigger picture, they invariably found that a challenge.

30 CU took the criticisms on the chin, knowing full well that what they did was different from the work conducted by ordinary commando units. There would inevitably be a learning curve, but at the same time, they had done much good. Of course, Commander Fleming told the Commodore the good news stories but unfortunately the bad ones would come home too. Not just the criticism about the 'Lessons Learnt' in the field, but also the amount of regular troops they had upset whilst conducting their business.

30 CU had the best of most things: with transport, daily equipment, they didn't feel the need to loot captured ports and towns like some other – albeit minority – troops. They became the victims of jealousy. This they largely ignored but some of the shit thrown did stick – as we will see later when General Patton had some choice words to say about them!

On 15 July it was learnt that 50th Northumberland Division had crossed the Semeta River and were advancing across the plain towards Catania, which was expected to fall in the immediate future. A field team was created from the Army section under Captain Martin-Smith, with Lieutenant Glanville and his RM orderly. Their duty was to penetrate the port of Catania. This did not go to plan as the 8th Durham Light Infantry and the Germans were fighting to reach the same destination and Martin-Smith and his men came across some fierce fighting.

30 CU joined the 8th Durham on the far side of Primosole Bridge beyond some farmhouses. It was at this stage that 30 CU's driver drove past the farmhouses and straight across the bridge under heavy fire towards Lentini ridges to get reinforcements. 30 CU, under the command of Lieutenant Colonel R. Lidwell, 8th Durhams, held for the bridge for twenty hours, after which, they returned to normal duties. It was a rare piece of typical commando action and was excellent for morale.

The lessons learnt from this escapade were the need for quality intelligence before going ahead to capture enemy documents. However, it was agreed that the Germans had acted quickly in their counter on this occasion and little warning was ever going to reach them ahead of confrontation. It was also agreed that the fall of Catania was going to take some time!

30 CU had to turn their attention elsewhere. Lieutenant Commander Riley heard that the US Seventh Army were having a peaceful time on the western side, with the fall of Marsala, Trapani and Palermo expected at any time. On 18 July, Captain Huntingdon-Whitely and Lieutenant Glanville took a team of RM with three despatch riders to Trapani. Two days later the Army section led by Captain Martin-Smith and Lieutenant

McFee left for Palermo (followed by Lieutenant Commander Riley and his RM orderly in a jeep).

The Troops didn't find their journey easy. Roads had been blasted to bits, Allied troops were crossing their paths, chaos was all around. When Glanville reached the American unit they were not sure if the cities had indeed fallen as the intelligence was confused. Something had to be done, though. Somehow a team of 30 CU managed to get into Trapani. Most documentation had been destroyed but they did find naval equipment of some significance.

What is interesting about this work is 30 CU's inability to deal with the amount of information they found there. They had been depleted to two commanding and eleven ORs, the Americans were occupied with thwarting looters in the city as well as other duties, so Italians troops, who had already surrendered, did the donkey work under 30 CU's watchful gaze. This did free up elements of 30 CU to explore Mount Erice (2,250 feet). Many stores of torpedoes and mines were found in caves on the way up, as well as a small Signals and WT station. When 30 CUs work was done the US 3rd Infantry Division guarded the loot for a while until provision could be made to move it all away.

Clearly, there were many lessons learnt from this little escapade but 30 CU knew they had made the best of what was a chaotic situation. There was no quiet spot anywhere on the island and, what with troops going this way and that, resistance fighting, looting, as well as pockets of commandos trying to make a decent fist of things, they had kept focused and done a sound job (managing to get the Americans to protect their captured equipment before returning home).

Commander Fleming was pleased with the news. He focused in on the intelligence gained, probably doing his best to ignore the action that 30 CU saw at Primosole Bridge (that was not the reason why they were in that area; but some action was inevitable). Perhaps in his own way, Fleming saw 30 CU as an intelligent commando unit, using their gadgets and brains rather than their fighting tactics to arrest important equipment and other intelligence. When, however, Fleming lost control of 30 CU to military establishments in the field, he was always cross with the inappropriate use of the unit, almost as if he was infuriated as to why 30 CU was to be used as regular soldiers – they were far too good to simply fight a war! This is why – to this day – veterans of 30 CU still praise Fleming so much: he put them on a pedestal like a proud father.

Despite all this, it was ascertained from the American troops that RMs within 30 CU hadn't pulled their weight and that vital information was not gathered from naval stores in Trapani, as specialist officers had followed 30 CU in and found much.

Mixed messages circulated around NID but it was concluded that 30 CU had made a difference. Although thinking on their feet, they had proved that their way of managing a forward commando unit had its uses. Indeed, a small pamphlet would be written for posterity by NID as to how to set up a unit such as 30 CU (referred to as 30 Assault Unit on the cover and therefore distributed approximately a year later).

30 CU had worked hard in Sicily. As a consequence sickness, accident and some minor casualties had seriously depleted the unit. This was made up slightly when the rear troops had arrived from North Africa. Lieutenant Commander Riley decided to regroup along the following lines:

1. Lieutenant McFee and Captain Martin-Smith, with the Army section, were transferred to the Dittsino River section in the expectation of being able to enter Catania with the 51st Highland or 5th Infantry Division.

2. Lieutenant Glanville and Captain Huntingdon-Whiteley, with his RMs, were instructed to remain with the US Seventh Army in its advance along the north coast with a view to entering Milazzo and Messina with the leading troops. Alternatively, in the event of this advance being halted, the team was to transfer to the Canadian front between Nicosia and Regalbuto to participate in any advance round the Etna massif, i.e. south to Catania or north to Taormina and Messina.

3. The remainder of the unit in Sicily was to remain at the Syracuse headquarters in order to be available to join in any rapid advance that might take place.

30 CU would not find the way forwards any easier than so far experienced. Lieutenant McFee and Captain Martin-Smith found a fresh German front before Catenanuovo. They were joined by the 78th Division from North Africa but after several days they were advised to return to Syracuse.

Lieutenant Glanville and Captain Huntingdon-Whiteley had advanced with the American 45th Division and likewise found fresh German troops; but also a shortage of petrol. 30 CU then moved across the Canadian front while the Americans re-equipped and regrouped.

Again, strong enemy resistance was met and it was decided that due to the lack of potential targets – equipment and other intelligence – 30 CU would return to Syracuse.

Chapter 8

A More Professional Unit

'In the Admiralty "Citadel", during the months before Normandy D-Day, we worked busily in an underground room.'

Arctic Snow to Dust of Normandy, Patrick Dalzel-Job

All the recent action had taught 30 CU and its officers some very important lessons about their core function. Also, teaming with the Americans (and some Canadians) had increased their skill in basic front-line fighting.

Perhaps one of the most important lessons learnt – and this was learnt from the Americans who searched captured intelligence stores after 30 CU – was the understanding that there was a severe lack of specialist officers within the unit. This was a major criticism because it was so difficult to get 30 CU in ahead of everyone else that compromises had to be made, and what was the point of being there if full advantage wasn't taken?

So more specialist personnel had to be introduced into the unit. The main problem with this was that the real specialists were not fighting men. That said, some existed and it was the remit of NID to ensure that this was fulfilled, and it was, in the guise of Lieutenant Commander F.A. Lincoln RNVR and Lieutenant J. Ogle RNVR, who were underwater weapons specialists. Two Admiralty scientists were also seconded to the unit, Mr A. Austen and Mr S.H. Taylor. They were made Lieutenant Commander and Lieutenant respectively. They then wasted no time in undertaking a full examination of the Naval stores at Syracuse, Augusta, Mellili and Trapani (which had already been given a thorough going over by 30 CU and the Americans).

The scientists found a lot of previously missed intelligence and this showed clearly the importance of attaching complete experts to the unit. A lesson learnt had found its solution and forever afterwards 30 CU/30 AU would have a pool of scientific experts to call upon. They had to be left back at 'base' and brought forwards when the need arose, but this was for two main reasons: first, the specialist's lack of military training; second, the specialist's importance to the British war effort and his need not to be captured – and consequently interrogated – by the enemy. The unit had carried out many interrogations themselves while in Syracuse and the enemy scientists *did* talk, so again, 30 CU learnt from their experiences and brought the specialists forwards when the need arose.

Lieutenant Commander Riley, perhaps with a new-found confidence, asked Lieutenant McFee to proceed to the American front and establish a permanent liaison with the US troops. He was well received initially, but once he reached their Headquarters he was told that he was not allowed to stay unless via a personal letter from General Alexander. This instruction came from Major General Koch who probably felt a little talked down to by the British officer. McFee left with his tail between his legs.

Once McFee was back at Syracuse he told Lieutenant Commander Riley, who instantly took the matter up with Fifteenth Army Group. He was told that it 'was in order' for elements of 30 CU to enter US areas. A signal was sent to Major General Koch requesting his permission for the unit to participate in the capture of Messina and Milazzo. Before any reply was received, both places had fallen and 30 CU had managed to enter Messina from the sea and the coast road under Eighth Army control. This irritated the Americans, but 30 CU had good reason to be there.

In truth 30 CU had been making up most of their excursions as they went along, muscling in where they thought they could do some good and the Allied forces had tolerated – occasionally welcomed – them but they did tread on several toes – like Major General Koch's; but this was inevitable!

What they began to appreciate was the need to ask permission at the highest level, to have their presence accepted as an operational tactic, or at least an important operational function, as a town, city, or port began to fall. It made sense to understand and feed back any intelligence and equipment of use along the way. This was universally accepted but how to implement such work was still largely unclear: when should 30 CU be activated? During the battle and then let them charge forwards or, once a situation had been taken and proved clear, then 30 CU and their team of specialists could run in and carry out their work quickly and efficiently.

The work pattern that we know of for 30 AU was established through these real-life conundrums. The trial and error, those depressing 'lessons learnt', had created a template for which the unit could work from. 30 CU were the forerunners to the more professional unit: 30 AU. That is the way to look at them today as the name change was instigated to reflect the new start. To jump from 'Commando Unit' to 'Assault Unit' was a more ambiguous title that took away the 'fighting unit' feel of the specialization they were in: commandos.

While all this was taking shape, the Eighth Army learned that part of 50th Division had reached the airfield to the south of Catania. Two teams were constructed to enter the city with assault troops. The first team was led by Captain Hargreaves-Heap and Lieutenant Orton. Their team consisted of RM ORs, while the other team was led by Captain Martin-Smith and Lieutenant Glanville, and consisted of two RM orderlies.

Before leaving Syracuse, street plans of Catania and maps of the surrounding country were carefully annotated with the latest intelligence available from Army headquarters and the local representatives of ISLD and ISRB. On the basis of this information a plan of action was drawn up whereby Lieutenant Orton, with half a section, was to handle the offices of the Port Authority and Italian Naval Headquarters. Captain Hargreaves-

Heap was to search the buildings, a lighthouse and lookout station to the south of the port, while Lieutenant Glanville and Captain Martin-Smith dealt first with the headquarters of the GAF and then dealt with the north side of the harbour (however when that was completed it was proposed that they should make their way to a reported German radar station on the headland of Ognina to the north of the city).

This kind of planning activity was indicative of the extra layer of detail the future 30 AU would meticulously calculate deep within the Citadel, in Whitehall. Perhaps the addition of the specialists had made the unit take extra strategic precautions to incorporate safe passage and clear access for these people once they were free to explore and capture the material they required. It seems logical and, as a consequence, the Syracuse experience was essential to the longevity of the unit. If Fleming and Godfrey had kept them in Whitehall, activating then on an as-and-when basis, they would never have grown to the extent they had done in the field and, as a consequence, would have been disbanded. After much persistence and heartache, the unit was now an asset within any front-line fighting force.

Politically NID had scored high with 30 CU. They had 'grown up in public' to a degree; but no one could dismiss the importance of their commando unit and the crucial intelligence it had gathered.

Chapter 9

All Shook Up

The party arrived at the bunkers before the city of Catania at 0500hrs on 6 August and joined up with the 8th Light Infantry.

It was found that the assault originally planned had been halted on the railway, which bordered the city, and only a few patrols succeeded in penetrating into the city and port areas. The neighbouring airfield had been extensively damaged in the fighting and fires were burning fiercely. It was therefore decided not to stop to make any examination of the wreckage but to press on into the city in order to seize the targets which had already been indicated. It is clear from this that the unit's extra layer of planning stood them in good stead, they had studied the maps and knew the area. It didn't matter that the goal posts had slightly changed now they were in theatre.

The four sub-sections of 30 CU advanced on their targets without delay. The enemy had ceased resistance in the city and were digging in on the rising ground in the northern suburbs. Streets and buildings were found to be extensively mined and many booby traps, most of them devised rather poorly, were encountered. The place was a death trap, but they had to press on.

The first target headquarters was captured quickly but little of interest was found. Lieutenant Glanville moved on to the second target headquarters but it was empty, having been moved by the Germans. However, a case of secret papers was found, which was later turned over to the RAF.

Captain Hargreaves-Heap dealt with Dopolavoro, where he discovered membership cards; he then moved on to the third target headquarters, which he found practically intact. He handed all his findings over to FSS.

By 1100hrs all parties had joined Lieutenant Orton in the harbour, which was being raised to the ground, burning buildings everywhere. The team carried out a search of the port and discovered some interesting data, most notably charts that related to the course of submarines in the straits of Gibraltar. Others papers related to movements of merchandise in the port and were despatched as being of possible interest to the Ministry of Economic Warfare. This is a good example of the diversity of documentation arrested by the unit.

The same evening, Lieutenants Orton and Glanville, along with a section of RMs, attempted to reach the WT station at Barriera del Bono, about 2 miles north west of Catania. This proved to be a little ambitious as they encountered a strong contingent of the enemy along the way. Early the next morning the same team successfully entered the WT station but found that it was only the Catania broadcaster and not of any military use. All they found was propaganda material.

The rest of the day was spent in exploring the Ognina area for the German radar station, which had been reported but not found. There was an AA battery and interesting equipment was recovered. It seems probable that the radar installation at this point was a small Wurzburg mounted on a limber and that it had been removed by the enemy by road. At the same time a villa in Catania was taken over as advanced headquarters to serve as a base for the advance up the coast.

It was noted that this exercise was the first ever to be searched systematically and according to the prearranged performance indicators, which had been based upon the most recent lessons learnt. That said, 30 CU was now a larger, more sophisticated unit than before, so their plans were easier to execute than before.

What is quite interesting about the recent campaign, however, was the lack of Naval intelligence captured. As we have seen, the most important documentation captured was for other

Marine Officers of 30 CU, Northampton, May 1944.

Staff Sergeant
Bramagh, Caen,
9 July 1944.
(Pen & Sword)

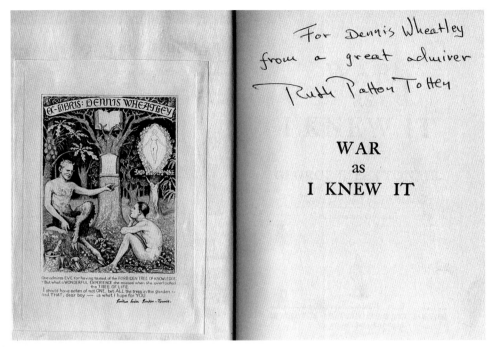

For Dennis Wheatley
from a great admirer
Ruth Patton Totten

WAR
as
I KNEW IT

Signed first edition of General Patton's posthumous memoirs, signed to Dennis Wheatley from the General's daughter. (*Author*)

Photograph and signature
of Patrick Dalzel-Job.
(*Author*)

Detail of The Citadel, hub of the intelligence gathering meetings of 30 NID. (*Author*)

Sitting alongside the Admiralty, The Citadel is an often overlooked building today; but during the Second World War it was the home of Ian Fleming's Red Indians. (*Author*)

Director of Naval Intelligence Rear Admiral John Godfrey, who kept 30 AU an RN reporting unit.

Commodore Rushbrooke, Godfrey's successor, dictates an instruction to his secretary.

Lt Cdr T.J. Glanville,
DSC, RNVR.

Marine Bill Wright, Caen, 1944. (*Pen & Sword*)

Capt H.O. Huntington-Whiteley, RM.

Charles Wheeler, 30 AU, searching a trashed vessel for vital intelligence. (*Pen & Sword*)

Clipped-winged Mark XVI Spitfire, typical of the aircraft that dive-bombed V2 rocket sites during Operation Big Ben. (*Graham A. Thomas*)

A limited edition print of Ted Poole's new sign for The Marine Public House. (*Ted Poole*)

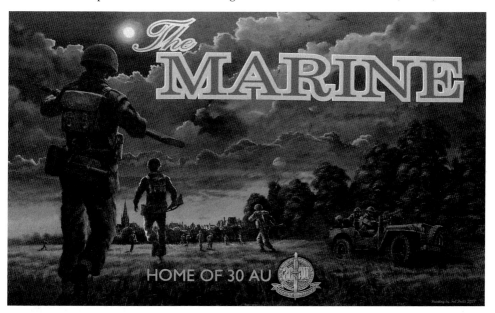

Blue plaque dedicated to 30 AU outside The Marine Public House, Littlehampton. (*Author*)

The Marine Public House today, spiritual home of 30 AU and their lasting memory. (*Author*)

government departments or services, such as the SOE or RAF. There was some concern that the unit was losing its prime objective, but that was just sabre-rattling from other government departments at NID's expense. The newly recruited technical experts – from the Admiralty – had conducted a thorough search of the Naval stores at Trapani, which had been kept secret from potential 'shareholders'. The result was a very rich harvest of information concerning enemy mining and mine-sweeper activity, along with important equipment, some of which was completely unknown to the Admiralty previously. This exercise really quashed the critics and proved 30 CU to be at the forefront of intelligence gatherers in the field (although this recovery was made more by luck than judgement as the target was not a core objective). That said, it really emphasized the value of specialists within the unit, despite the good fortune of the whole loot being overlooked by the US units that passed through first!

After Catania, two teams under Captains Martin-Smith, Hargreaves-Heap and Lieutenant Glanville joined up with 169 Brigade to advance up the coast to Messina. Progress was slow because of landmines and persistent German rearguard, who took pot shots along the ridges that ran down from Mount Etna.

Acireale fell on 8 August, where a German ordnance factory was captured that contained spare parts for an 88mm gun and related documentation. 30 CU then moved forward towards Giarre and Riposto (jointly Jonia). This was a place of great interest to 30 CU because it housed the shadow headquarters from Augusta. The road was not easy. Not only were there many landmines along the way, the German defence made progress as slow as 2 miles a day, at best.

On 9 August the two sections of 30 CU joined 169 Brigade and attempted to reach the outskirts of Giarre ahead of the pack. As a consequence they came under heavy attack from the enemy, which led to enemy tanks and artillery being thrown into the fray. 30 CU didn't suffer any casualties but 169 Brigade did, causing great concern and 30 CU were told firmly to exert maximum caution in the future as the casualties were extremely high and they were responsible.

30 CU decided to transfer to the coastal section where 6th Light Infantry were advancing against strong opposition. Through sheer determination the unit entered Riposto at 1500hrs on 12 August, ahead of the general advance. By 1700hrs they had reached the Vennero River, which marked the northern boundary of the town. They encountered strong resistance from the enemy so retired to the town and made a complete search. A small WT station was discovered on the quay and a GAF headquarters, which was reported to the RAF.

This was not glamorous work, and was hot and sweaty. The enemy was hiding out everywhere, the landmines were placed in surprisingly cunning places and the intelligence/equipment captured was not exactly sensational. It was time to move on.

The next two days were spent advancing slowly towards Mascali and Fiumefreddo. Large areas had been – or were being – demolished and 30 CU found the restrictions challenging to say the least. The two teams came together and devised a slow but effective way through the carnage: Lieutenant Glanville rode on the back of Private Heath's bike and carried on by foot once through the rubble. The rest of the unit followed suit.

By this means Giardini was reached with the leading troops, despite more landmines. The unit reached the joint German and Italian headquarters in the group of hotels at Teormina on 15 August.

The headquarters had been cleared by the Germans before evacuation and the team decided to bring the rest of 30 CU together at the headquarters before conducting a thorough search of the surrounding area. This was completed the following day and found very little except a map of Europe showing where the main GAF homing beacons were plotted. The map was disguised as sheet music atop a piano in the GAF Officers' Mess. This would be important intelligence for the RAF.

As soon as Taormina had been completely checked, 30 CU decided to push towards Messina. With lengthy stretches of the coast road demolished by shellfire, the only way forwards was by foot. An attempt was made to make a passage of 21 miles over the mountains on foot but German sentries were found and the route was considered impractical due to the large amounts of ammunition – at least – deemed necessary to obtain safe passage (also 30 CU didn't want a reoccurrence of the last situation involving 169 Brigade). So the only way to reach Messina was by sea. 30 CU retired to the new advance headquarters at Riposto, while Lieutenant Glanville and Captain Martin-Smith went to SS Brigade Headquarters to see if it was possible to land a party of 30 CU at – or near – Messina.

Glanville was told that two LCIs were waiting at Giardini to take members of 2 and 3 Commando to a point on the mainland to the south of Reggio Calabria and that it would order for a small party of 30 CU to take part if room could be found to accommodate them in the boats. Due to a lack of credible objective once at Messina (i.e. a credible reason for going in the first place!) Major P. Young DSO MC, officer commanding the raid, said that there was no room for 30 CU.

Next, an application was made to headquarters in Augusta for a suitable craft to make the trip, but this was turned down on the basis that coastal craft had recently experienced heavy losses through shellfire from coastal batteries on the mainland. Coastal forces craft were therefore ordered not to attempt the passage of the straits until the enemy gun positions had been silenced. Also, the power-that-be were probably wary of 30 CU and wanted nothing to hinder the operations already being carried out by other units.

However, a lift was eventually obtained for a detachment of 30 CU to land with a truck at Scaletta. The objective: to reach Messina by road. Before embarking it was learned that elements of the US Seventh Army had already reached Messina. 30 CU now knew from experience that the Americans would want passes in order for them to operate in that area. Slightly cavalier-like, the unit decided to move forwards and worry about that later!

The landing took place at midnight on 15/16 August, with the outskirts of Messina reached three and a half hours later. The road was obstructed by broken bridges and mines, but Private Edwards, the driver of the vehicle, safely negotiated all these obstacles and, after coming under shellfire from across the straits, brought his vehicle to a sober stop in the shelter of the dock area.

The town and port were deserted having been bombed by the RAF two nights previously and entered the previous afternoon by the Americans; but the Americans soon left after experiencing heavy shelling.

The whole area was a maze of booby traps, depth charges, AP and AT mines, but this didn't deter 30 CU. Reinforced by a team of RMs, headed by Captain Hargreaves-Heap, the unit made a thorough search of the town and surrounding area.

A vast quantity of valuable material was found in wrecked vehicles and demolished buildings. The most important discoveries being: working drawings of the GAMMA system of remote power control for anti-aircraft guns, a collection of identity cards and personal history booklets belonging to the 1st Parachute Battalion, as well as the battalion administration papers and manual on parachute jumping, a number of frequency tables for field RT and WT links used by the German Army.

Certain documents were of great importance and of immediate use by the 8th Army Headquarters. Other documents found their way to the RAF.

A team of 30 CU progressed to the mountain road, which they searched for two days finding some interesting items along the way. Meanwhile, the port party had been engaged in clearing the harbour of obstacles and mines. In all 271 depth charges were rendered safe by the team. 30 CU assisted this exercise, disarming many booby traps. The port party suffered severe casualties from the explosion of a depth charge they were handling. 30 CU had no losses, although one party had a narrow escape when a RM OR was prevented from playing with the controls of a radio set that was found to be connected to a charge of guncotton.

While this work was in progress, shelling from across the straits became more intense, some 1,200 shells falling in the course of about 20 hours. An effort was made to move certain interesting pieces of naval equipment which were lying around the harbour, into air-raid shelters or other strongly constructed buildings. At the same time a number of Italian dockyard workers were traced and interrogated in regard to the location of naval stores, which had been dispersed to secret hideouts in the Messina area.

The party having returned from Cape Peloro, where the WT had been found destroyed, 30 CU decided to make their way back to advanced headquarters. Their truck had been damaged in an accident, so the badly shaken unit made their way back on foot and then by boat, as the British artillery had infiltrated the hillside. It was largely due the increased presence of the British artillery that Lieutenant Glanville returned with Mr Austin, Mr Taylor and some RM orderlies, to make a tour of all the naval installations around Messina.

In the various establishments they visited, much hardware and documentation regarding torpedoes was discovered, which they found most interesting. It was also established that torpedoes were being housed in the basement of an Italian tuberculosis hospital. 30 CU was told that the Whitehead 18" torpedoes had been thrown off a cliff but they were later found in the hollow of a tree! This was all quality naval intelligence.

While the north-east tip of the island was being cleared up, the remainder of the unit was engaged in repairing vehicles and preparing weapons and stores for Operations BAYTOWN and AVALANCHE, i.e. the Allied landing at Reggio Calabria and Salerno. 30 CU was allocated as follows: Lieutenant Commander Riley, Lieutenant Glanville, Captain Martin-Smith (with the Army section and twelve RM ORs) to take part on the assault on Salerno beaches; Lieutenant Davies, with his RM orderly, to join Eighth Army Headquarters to participate in the assault on Reggio Calabria, then to accompany the advance northwards and to report on any targets encountered; Captain Ward to bring 'B' echelon to Salerno on D+2; Captain Hargreaves-Heap to remain in Sicily with the headquarters section; Lieutenant Commander Curtis, who was sick, to return home as soon as possible.

Chapter 10

30 CU Assessment

'I was in the Army then. We were under Monty in
Eighth Corps.'

For Your Eyes Only, Ian Fleming

It is clear that the Admiralty was happy with the work of 30 CU
at the conclusion of their work in Sicily; but 30 CU had managed
to annoy a lot of people along the way. They had flown by the
seat of their pants and muscled in on other operations that had
been meticulously planned and, in fairness, most outfits had
been happy to accommodate them as much as possible; but 30
CU had outstayed their welcome on more than one occasion.
Winston Churchill knew this – it was nothing new – as he wrote
in vol. II of *The Second World War*: 'Throughout the summer and
autumn [1940] I wished to help the Secretary of State for War in
his conflict with War Office and Army prejudice about the
Commandos.' The problems NID experienced with other
government departments and the teething problems with 30 CU
were just the norm to a large extent. It's true that they needed to
show that their way of doing things had great merits, but while
achieving – broadly – that, they had caused problems and, more
unforgiveable, they had caused some casualties in the field.

The lessons learnt by the Admiralty concerning the work of 30
CU thus far were officially:

1. The intelligence briefing provided by NID was 'distinctly

scanty', with only basic plans being drawn up within Whitehall.

2. Arising from the foregoing, no priority lists were drawn up to show the priority of items to be captured.
3. The unit still possessed no means of communication, and was therefore forced to rely on networks operated by the various clandestine organizations. Apart from other considerations this was not practical in view of the difficulty of maintaining a continuous liaison with the headquarters concerned.
4. Shortages of motor transport, as a result of which a disproportionate number of men were employed on the repair and servicing of captured vehicles. Much time and trouble might have been saved if the unit had been able to operate its own coastal craft.
5. There was a general dispersal of effort. There was a limited number of high-grade targets in Sicily which were likely to satisfy immediate requirements. It was considered that all available manpower should have been allocated to their exploitation.
6. The discipline and training for 30 CU work displayed by the RM Troop was substantially below the standard necessary for a unit of this importance.

Certain things could be addressed straight away and Commander Fleming ensured that he personally did just that. He was the man who obtained some of the best equipment for 30 CU to perform their tasks, and also helped secure the Citadel as a place where the unit could plan their own strategies as NID 30 before taking them into the field as 30 AU (see Part 2).

When I interviewed veterans from 30 AU while researching this book and its sister work *Ian Fleming's Secret War*, they told me that although they never met Ian Fleming (because they were not officers), they knew that he was working on their behalf behind the scenes. They managed to get a very impressive fleet of vehicles and craft, which many people agree was solely down to Commander Fleming's persistence and instance.[1]

Fleming knew that in order to make a success of 30 CU, user

manuals had to be written and printed, hence the need for a notebook of priorities when it came to the capture of documentation and equipment (and revised edition), also Godfrey would take a hand in writing a document about 'How to Create an Intelligence Gathering Commando Unit'. Godfrey had done similar things before,[2] as he firmly believed in working from everybody else's experiences, good and bad, as it saved time and moved things forwards at a greater pace.[3]

Godfrey didn't tolerate bad vibes. He insisted that if fellow officers had problems with each other (to do with the nature of their work) that they meet each other face to face, sort the damned thing out and then go into print with the outcome! He didn't like negativity and dismissed it, which some officers found a little unfeeling at times. Godfrey knew, however, that fallings-out cost time and that was something NID had precious little of.

So what else did NID learn from their commando unit? The need for attaching specialist officers and Admiralty scientists to the unit; the need for linguists or officers possessing a good grasp of Italian, German, Spanish and French. At the beginning of the campaign only one officer spoke Italian, although several others grasped the fundamentals of the language as time went on.

One direct criticism – that had nothing to do with lessons learnt – was the stupid behaviour displayed by ORs, such as failing to observe the rules of dress and conduct when operating in the US area and showing a generally slovenly bearing when off duty. This was unforgivable, but something that had been present from the very beginning within the RM Troop. Couple that with the criticism/lesson learnt with regard to the RM Troop (as detailed above), there was much criticism – blame – on this aspect of 30 CU.

With much good work taken into account and common sense solution being worked into the mix quickly, the lessons learnt were finally summarized as follows:

1. That small field teams, consisting of two officers and six to

eight ORs are adequate, when properly trained and briefed, to exploit most Naval intelligence targets and at the same time small enough to be able to operate in front line areas without causing annoyance or embarrassment to Army formations.
2. That on the other hand there was an urgent requirement for adequate numbers of troops for guarding targets in areas captured, but not cleared and settled.
3. That the best results can be obtained by operating in three echelons, i.e. First, an assault party to capture, search and assess the target, Second, a guard party to protect it particularly against the depredations of Allied troops, and Third, a technical party of specialists officers and scientists, to be called forwards by the first echelon according to the 'nature and value of the target'.

It was pragmatism like this that rapidly enhanced 30 CUs capabilities, along with Commander Fleming and his two separate bosses (DNIs). That said, it is interesting to note that in his posthumous memoirs (*War As I Knew It*, The Riverside Press, 1947), General George Patton wrote of 'Small Unit Tactics' – that they should seldom be split but, if they were, that they should be 'capable of mutual support'. He also mentioned that speed was essential for a small team's success. This was a concern for 30 CU, especially when they had to return to base to pick up specialists who were not in any way commandos but were imperative to the analysis of any documents that they would acquire.

Through his words, Patton did highlight some of 30 CU's frustrations; that said, they would probably disagree with his thoughts concerning an infantry squad: 'the life of the infantry squad depends on its capacity of fire. It must fire.' There were occasions when 30 CU had to act like a small infantry squad but the one thing they always tried to avoid was to fire – if they did, the element of surprise would disappear; not that that would bother 'Old Blood and Guts' Patton of course. The work of 30 CU was quite typically British in that respect.

Chapter 11

Southern Italy

'His other hand went to Bond's shoulder. "Our Commissioner's got a motto: Never send a man where you can send a bullet." You might remember that. So long, Commander.'

For Your Eyes Only, Ian Fleming

30 CU had been split up through Operations BAYTOWN and AVALANCHE, although maintaining their prime purpose of gathering intelligence and equipment.

On 3 September, Lieutenant Davies took part in the assault on Reggio Calabria. Instead of carrying out his normal duties, he was called upon to take charge of the navigation of certain amphibious craft that had got into difficulties.[1]

Davies took the matter in hand and guided several groups of these craft ashore without loss, for which he was commended by the Army authorities.

After the landing, Lieutenant Davies accompanied the advance of Eighth Army for some distance up the Italian peninsula, but as he did not encounter any intelligence targets of value, he returned to base and travelled to Salerno by sea, arriving on 18 September.

30 CU were not effective during this period, a good example being the missed opportunity at Taranto and Termoli, which was rich with Naval Intelligence, but not searched by anyone from the unit.

On 10 September, Lieutenant Commander Riley and his team

passed through Salerno, reaching the village of Vietri at 1000hrs. This was a positive step as the day before they were considerably hindered in their landing because their ship had hit a sandbank, which damaged the vehicle release door and waterlogged their vehicles. But now they were back on the road.

Targets were located in a series of houses occupied by railway employees. 30 CU found secret papers burning on arrival. The terms of the Italian Armistice were not known to the officers of 30 CU, otherwise action might have been taken against the Italian staff for breaking them so seriously. The fires were put out but little of interest was salvaged.

As the Germans appeared to be present in the hills in strength, the position was consolidated with the headquarters of the Special Services Brigade, which had been set up in the village, and with Nos 2 and 41 RM Commandos, who were holding the pass. 30 CUs base was set up in the former Italian Naval Headquarters referred to above.

At about midday, a party consisting of Captain Martin-Smith and four ORs of the Army section, accompanied by Lieutenant Glanville, set out to reconnoitre the plain inland from the beaches, the objective being a WT or communications centre that had been reported in the area. The party succeeded in penetrating some miles inland, and although the enemy were sighted on several occasions, no shots were exchanged. The Germans seemed mildly curious and showed no inclination to respond to the intrusion. The objective could not be traced, so it is probable either that the equipment in question was transportable or that the original report had confused the pylons of the electricity supply grid with WT aerial masts.

No documents or equipment were captured on this occasion but it was noted how easy it was to explore a town shortly after an invasion before a counter-attack could be implemented!

It became apparent over the next two days that the unit was wasting their time in Salerno. It had never been a naval stronghold and the lack of interesting documentation and equipment found enhanced this perception.

As 30 CU knitted itself back together, it became apparent that the enemy counter-attack was getting stronger. The area around Vietri was coming under heavy bombardment by accurate mortar and machine-gun fire. To add to this, groups of enemy troops appeared from cellars and smashed buildings in the dead of night to attack Allied positions. 30 CU attempted to continue its searches but walked into a full battalion while trying to locate an enemy WT post. The unit quickly withdrew and reported the presence to a fellow Army unit which was in danger of being cut off.

It was sound judgement that Lieutenant Commander Riley decided to take on other targets in the Naples area; there was little else they could in the intensity of the Salerno war zone, however.

On the night of 11/12 September, an armed reconnaissance of the beaches and outlets was carried out between Castellammare Stabia and Torre Annunziata. This recon was accomplished under Lieutenant Commander Riley by a team consisting of Captain Martin-Smith and eight ORs from the Army and RM sections (with Lieutenant Berncastle and a team of regular Naval personnel). The object of the recon was to bring back information to decide the feasibility of a surprise landing point some 25 miles behind the enemy. The task was carried out successfully with no casualties.

The following day Riley made his report on the reconnaissance to Commodore Oliver RN, by whom he was informed that the capture of Capri had been entrusted to Commander Wybird RN, and that 30 CU was requested to provide a party to deal with any intelligence targets on the island.

Riley was pleased to do such a thing and must have noted that 30 CU's work was being appreciated from many different corners now. The teething problems had been ironed out and a way forwards was clear. He formed a team comprising an Army section and seven RM ORs commanded by Captain Martin-Smith and accompanied by Lieutenant Glanville. The party was completed by Lieutenant G. Taylor RN, a gunnery officer who had been detailed to report upon the coastal batteries on the island, and a signalman. The expedition sailed under the overall command of Commander Wybird.

The small harbour at Capri (to the south of the island) was approached before dawn on 13 September; the enemy was nowhere in sight. The Troop was therefore taken around the island to the large harbour. Here a landing was made shortly after dawn and no resistance was encountered. In fact, the party were met by the Capri town anti-fascist committee, from whom it was learned that an extensive neo-fascist organization, led by one Maresciallo Guido Salverini, was in occupation of the upper island, with its headquarters in the lighthouse and lookout station above Anacapri.

The landing party was accordingly divided into two teams, the first, consisting of 3 RM ORs under Lieutenant Commander Riley, to handle the coastguard station above Capri, while the second comprised the rest of the party to deal with neo-fascists.

Riley met with no opposition at the coastguard station, where he captured information of some interest.

The others had commandeered a lorry and, accompanied by a guide – provided by the anti-fascist council – dismounted near the Villa San Michele. After a brief reconnaissance the force split into three small teams and, approaching the objective from all sides, captured the blackshirt military men as they were washing and dressing. Salverini's sleeping cabin in the lighthouse was taken intact, and from a small safe a number of interesting documents and material were recovered, including a clandestine WT set, the list of the names and addresses of the members of a post-occupational organization in the Naples area and certain other papers classified Top Secret. Salverini himself was picked up later in the day by a patrol on Monte Tiberio. He was shipped to X Corps as a POW and his private Army disarmed and brought under control.

30 CU then discovered a store of dossiers on the residents of Capri and the neighbouring islands. By 1700hrs all the intelligence targets had been thoroughly searched, just in time for the US Naval delegation's arrival under Captain Andrews USN!

That night a conference was held where it was decided to capture the island of Ischia at dawn the next morning. It was also agreed that use should be made of a flotilla of three Italian ships that were lying in Capri harbour.

A plan was therefore drawn up for a party to sail from Capri at 0400hrs the next day (14 September) in order to land on Ischia before first light. A team of 30 CU, consisting of Captain Martin-Smith with his Army section and eight RM ORs, prepared for the operation. Lieutenant Glanville would command this group, whose duty it was to identify intelligence targets and round up any neo-fascist or other post-occupational organizations on the island.

The first objective was the Albergo Roma, a small hotel at St Angel, which according to Italian intelligence sources housed a clandestine WT set. It was therefore decided to search this area first, without climbing the cliffs to the radar jamming and lookout stations (since no recent intelligence was available in regard to the strength and disposition of the defence of these objectives). After the hotel and surrounding buildings had been searched, it was decided to proceed direct to Porto D'Ischla.

The landing party of 30 CU therefore joined forces with a US Naval party, which included Commander Kramer USN, Lieutenant Commander Douglas Fairbanks Jr., USNR (the actor) and Mr John Steinbeck (the novelist).[2]

The flotilla arrived at St Angelo at 0500hrs and from there they made the tricky journey ashore, navigating submerged rocks and the steep slope of the beach. The hotel was searched but apart from the German manageress and some anti-gas warfare material, nothing of interest was captured.

The landing at St Angelo having been delayed, it was late in the day before Porto D'Ischia was reached. In the town it was established that the fascist militia was still under arms. It was further stated that a number of Germans from the radar and WT stations were still at large in the woods on Mt Epomeo, or were living in disguise in the villages. At 1000hrs a US Naval party arrived to take over the island, but withdrew a few hours later as their strength was considered insufficient to hold the island in the event of a neo-fascist uprising. 30 CU were left in charge of the island by the US Naval captain and set up headquarters in the naval barracks in the port.

The unit now faced a selection of very different responsibilities other than intelligence gathering: policing duties for everyone on the island, a satisfactory liaison with the Italian Armed Forces who had come over to the Allied side, maintaining the level and supervising the distribution of civilian food supplies. It was all akin to British Armed Forces in Kosovo at the turn of the twenty-first century; but then again, fundamental life issues don't ever change much. Suffice to say, the diverse work 30 CU did at Porto became a shining example of the diverse work an intelligence unit should be prepared to undertake.

On 15 September, Lt Glanville sailed to the island of Procida accompanied by Lt Berncastle, gunnery officer Lieutenant Taylor and his team. The objects of the operation were for Berncastle's party to make a reconnaissance of the beaches and of the harbour of the island, and to survey all the shipping; for Taylor to inspect coastal defence batteries and 'get the guns into firing order'; and for Glanville to handle intelligence objectives on the island.

Procida was found to be free of German troops, although a number of MVSN were still at large and under arms. The port and harbour officials proved most cooperative. It was learned that a party of OSS officers, under Captain Frank Tarullo, had been landed two evenings previously and had installed themselves as an advanced intelligence post, their objectives: to observe movements of ships in the Procida channel and troop movements on the mainland; and to interrogate refugees and others arriving from the Naples area.

The OC of the party proved to be most helpful and co-operative, and furnished a list of the more interesting refugees. Amongst these was the name of the accountant employed by the SIC Torpedo works at Baia. Interrogated by Lieutenant Glanville, he furnished full details and plans of the complex of factories, storehouses and testing ranges between Monte Procida and Baia. He also mentioned that all these plants had been prepared for demolition and stated that Admiral Minisini, the general manager and technical director of SIC, was being held by the Germans in his house on the testing range. Apparently it was their intention to ship him to Berlin as soon as possible.

Lieutenant Taylor met with a good deal of passive resistance in connection with the coastal batteries. First it was stated that all the breech blocks were missing. When these were found it was discovered that the obturators had been buried. Finally Taylor decided to return with the rest of the party in order to co-opt some more willing Italian assistance.

Vice Admiral J.A.V. Morse RN had taken the appointment as Flag Officer Western Italy (FOWIT) and had moved into temporary headquarters at Capri. On the evening of 16 September, FOWITs SOO paid a visit to Ischia and informed 30 CU that they were free to operate in the area if they gave twenty-four hours' notice of operations, either through SOO to FOWIT or on to NOIC Ischia, when that position should be filled. As an urgent requirement, permission was given for an immediate raid against the torpedo firing range at San Martino in order to remove Admiral Minisini and to capture documents and, possibly, material relating to recent torpedo practice. And most importantly, anything connected with the new midget submarine.

It was also in their remit to prevent, if possible, the demolition of the plants and stocks of ready use torpedoes. The operation was laid on to commence at 1330hrs on 17 September, when the moonlight was favourable.

At 2100hrs on the 16th, a report was received from the OSS that German E-boats were at sea. Two Italian companies had been taken out to clear the whole area.[3] No E-boat was sighted, the only prey being a small motorboat full of refugees. These people were interrogated as to enemy troop movements and conditions in Naples. From the nature of these replies it appears that several of them were German agents who had been sent to spread rumours of enemy troop concentrations and epidemics of cholera in Naples.

Further sensational reports, mainly relating to movements of E-boats or to alleged coastal defences on the mainland, were also received about this time. These reports were considered in detail, but in the absence of any corroboration, it was decided that they could only be proved or disproved by actual reconnaissance. It should be mentioned that these OSS officers were all first-generation Americans or of Neapolitan origin had been selected for their language qualifications and had, in most instances, received little or no training in intelligence work.

The next day was spent in preparing for and planning the operation against the torpedo range at San Martino. This was not an easy task in view of the conflicting intelligence reports available. In view of the possibility of encountering strong defences and numerous enemy, it was decided to rely on speed and surprise. For this purpose an up-to-date craft was selected, fitted with a special silent underwater exhaust and capable of a speed of 38 knots in a calm sea. This plan entailed the additional advantage of the presence of the Italian officers who might be relied on to assist smooth and silent working in the event of Admiral Minisini, who was reported to be strongly anti-British, offering any resistance. Naturally the Italians could not be fully briefed as to the intended operations, although they willingly volunteered for any form of hazardous service.

The party selected for the raid consisted of Lieutenant Glanville (as OC), Captain Martin-Smith with the Army section, Lieutenant Berncastle and six RM ORs. The landing party was arranged as follows: a team comprising Glanville and Martin-Smith, with Corporal Ellington RM, Lance Corporal Blake RM and Private Edwards (King's Liverpool Regiment), to handle the Admiral and his companions; a search party was arranged under Sergeant Whitby to look for documents; a fire support party under Sergeant Whyman RM, and Lieutenant Berncastle and two RMs to keep charge of the boat and supervise its navigation.

The night of the 17th was calm with a low-lying mist. The craft slid noiselessly alongside the jetty at the range and the landing party were ashore before the presence of the boat was noted (except by an Italian watchman who did not raise the alarm).

A number of Italian workmen were quickly rounded up and interrogated. They undertook to guide a party to where Admiral Minisini was sleeping. The fire support party trained their weapons on areas where hostile fire was possible, their orders being to open fire the moment the Germans showed any signs of coming to life.

Admiral Minisini was soon located and interviewed by Lieutenant Glanville, to whom he declared that he would not move, save under compulsion. He was therefore declared a POW upon which the Admiral agreed to come without more ado, except for a request to be allowed to pack his belongings and to be accompanied by his wife. Signora Minisini, who was reliably reported to hold strong pro-German sympathies, was dealt with by Captain Martin-Smith, whose German was perfect. So much so that the Signora was under the impression that she was being removed by the Germans and kept referring to him as 'this charming young Rhinelander'. Eventually the Admiral and his wife were taken aboard the boat and sent to Ischia, where they passed the night. They were then taken onwards to Capri.

Chapter 12

An Admiral's Interrogation and its Consequences

'He came out looking like a Red Indian with blue-grey eyes.
Just before midnight he quietly opened the side door into the
automobile bay, got into the Plymouth and drove off on the last
lap south of Relighsburg.'

For Your Eyes Only, Ian Fleming

At Capri next morning Admiral Minisini was interrogated by the staff of FOWIT and also by 30 CU. He explained that all the documents relating to recent Italian torpedo research and to the development of the midget submarine were stored in various places indicated by him in the buildings on and near the torpedo range. He also mentioned that important tests with experimental torpedoes were being conducted by the Germans at the Silurificio Whitehead SA Fiume. A signal was therefore sent to the OC 30 CU suggesting that the underwater weapons specialists should come to Ischia as soon as possible.

It was decided that the recovery of the documents mentioned by Admiral Minsini was sufficiently important to justify the mounting of a second raid the same night (18/19 September). It was appreciated that after the last show there was a considerable risk of the landing party meeting with a warm reception and special precautions were taken to cope with this contingency. It was further decided to carry out a reconnaissance of the country inland from San Martino, since a signal had been received from COIS Med, indicating the radar and communications centre at Licola as an important target. Intelligence reports received from the OSS indicated that the area was strongly defended, although 30 CUs experiences up to that time hadn't confirmed that as fact. It was therefore arranged to make an armed patrol of the area while the buildings on the torpedo range were being searched. An additional objective of the raid was to locate the guns that had been shelling Ischia and Procida during the day.

In view of its low maximum speed of 16 knots and the noise of its exhaust, it was decided not to go alongside but to tow the landing party in a whaler to a point near the objective and to lay off while they rowed ashore. A fire party of RMs was arranged. The landing party was organized in three teams, one to make a preliminary survey of the buildings (then to climb the cliff and identify and observe the enemy positions), a second to search the positions already indicated by Admiral Minisini and a third to give covering fire in an emergency.

The landing party got ashore without incident, although most of the men were seasick, the whaler having moved a good deal in the choppy sea. The Italian workers on the range were immediately lined up and placed under armed guard in a room adjacent to the entrance to the tunnel leading to Baia. The places where the documents were stored were identified and handed over to a search party consisting of Corporal Shermuly and Lance Corporal Mayers of the Army section, who undertook a meticulous search of the offices and laboratory. The opportunity was also taken to carry out some useful counter-demolition work.

The patrol party, consisting of Lieutenant Glanville, Captain Martin-Smith, Sergeant Whitby, Corporal Ellington, Lance Corporal Blake RM, and Private Edwards, climbed the cliff to Monte Procida and patrolled the whole area for an hour. The coastal batteries reported on Monte Procida were found to be non-existent, although marks on the road indicated that certain of the shells falling on Ischia came from self-propelled guns specially brought up from the plain. This fact was later

confirmed by Italian civilian sources. MG posts were noted at
Torre Gaveta and San Martino. It was intended to make a further
reconnaissance towards Licola, but this was precluded by the
rising of the moon, the weather being clear. The patrol returned
therefore to the torpedo range and, after the officers had satisfied
themselves that a meticulous search had been made, the
captured documents were packed into sacks and the landing
party embarked in the whaler reaching their craft without
incident. Once again the Germans had shown no sign of life.

The next morning Taylor and Austin arrived in Ischia in order
to examine documents captured from the torpedo range and to
interrogate Admiral Minisini.

For clarity, the strength of 30 CU in Naples was as follows:

1. A base headquarters in Salerno harbour under Lieutenant
   McFee.
2. A team consisting of Lieutenant Orton, with three RM ORs,
   who were waiting to enter Naples by road in a truck. Their
   objective to handle intelligence targets for the leading troops
   in the port area and to work their way through to the
   objectives around the Campi Flegrei.
3. The advanced party on the island of Ischia.

Lieutenant Orton's party were still held up by the military
situation, since, although elements of the Eighth Army had
joined up with the Americans of the Fifth Army near Controne,
the general movement of the front inland was east from Salerno
towards Eboli, rather than through the Vietri pass to Naples.

The advanced party, on the other hand, was still able to move
around by sea and was faced with a substantial number of
targets to handle. The most important being: Baia – the SIC
torpedo factory; Lake Lucrene – the German torpedo depot;
Pozzuoli – armaments plant; Bagnara – steelyards; Licola – radar
station and communication centre; Lago Della Patria and Nisida
– seaplane bases; Castellamare Stabbia – shipyards.

In addition, there were a number of industrial targets of lesser
importance as well as security targets, the most significant of

which was the German Army command headquarters in the Albergo Dei Cesari at Lake Lucrene.

Operations around Monte Procida had proved the feasibility of small raiding parties penetrating to targets located in coastal areas. The only serious obstacles envisaged were the fact that little was known in regard to recent enemy minelaying activities (minefields existing before the date of the Italian Armistice had been declared by the local Italian Naval authorities), and the shortage of current and reliable intelligence on enemy troop movements and dispositions. The principal source of such intelligence up to this time had been the OSS forward party on Procida. Their reports had proved to be so unreliable that it was finally decided that armed reconnaissance of the targets in view was essential before any major operation was mounted.

On the morning of the 19 September, a small team set out from Ischia to patrol the roads off the Licolese in order to observe any troop movements that might be taking place on the main coast road (Torre Gaveta, Monte Cuma, Licola), and also to note the positions of any coastal defences. The craft selected was small and made a poor target for shore-based guns. The party comprised Lieutenant Berncastle OC, a COPP party under Lieutenant Hamilton, four ORs of 30 CU under Captain Martin-Smith and Lieutenant Glanville. Accurate observations were made of movements of troops and armour on the road, but the patrol came to an abrupt end when the craft broke a crankshaft. Volunteers swam ashore and arranged for an Italian motorboat to tow the disabled craft to Ischia. Fortunately the Germans ignored this sitting target.

In the afternoon Glanville travelled to Capri in order to report to FOWIT, who gave permission for further operations to be carried out in the Naples area. A US craft was leaving Capri harbour to return to Ischia, when the senior US Naval officer signalled the boat to investigate a suspicious-looking sailing vessel that was approaching the mainland. The target was quickly overhauled and was found to be carrying out a clandestine operation for OSS. Her papers being apparently in order she was allowed to proceed. The US craft therefore turned away towards Ischia, but soon came under heavy fire from the German coastal batteries and SP guns on Cape Miserno. When a splinter from a near miss penetrated the boat's side and jammed the steering gear, the craft could only steam astern. She was making good progress when further near misses caused casualties amongst the crew, after which the careless handling of a smoke float set fire to the aft gasoline tank. The fire was extinguished but several of the crew suffered severe burns, from which three Italians subsequently died – an unnecessary loss of life all things considered. The boat reached Porto D'Ischia about two hours later, but was too badly damaged to be of any further use.

Chapter 13

Further Work in Southern Italy

'"Damn M! Damn you! Damn the whole silly service!" There
were angry tears in the voice. "You're just a lot of children
playing at Red Indians. Taking these people on by yourself! It's
– it's showing off. That's all it is. Showing off."'

From a View to a Kill, Ian Fleming

The next morning a patrol was carried out in a small Italian
motorboat. The route followed was much the same as that of the
previous morning. Considerable movements of troops were
observed on the inland road near Lake Fusaro towards Monte
Cuma. Due to good weather and no moonlight, it was decided
to carry out an armed reconnaissance towards Licola to assess
the amount of enemy resistance in the area.

Captain Heap had arrived with reinforcements – Royal
Marines – but Captain Martin-Smith had gone sick with
'complete exhaustion'. Martin-Smith was recommended to rest
for two to three weeks.

The Admiralty scientists had spent the past two days going
through the documents that had been removed from the torpedo
testing range at San Martino and the interrogation of Admiral
Minisini at Capri. Their meticulous analysis was used to plan an
operation against the SIC factory at Haia.

An armed patrol was made ready that very evening:
Lieutenant Glanville, with a landing party of six ORs, with
support from 12 Royal Marines from LCI (L) 249. The operation

started at 2300hrs and stood off Monte Procida thirty minutes later. The MG post sent up warning flares and a brief exchange of fire took place, the enemy guns being silenced almost immediately by the heavy concentration of fire from the ship. This did not last, as the raging battle activated enemy positions further along the coast and the small vessel was soon under heavy fire. A 50mm anti-tank shell passed through the engine room without causing any damage or casualties and the ship was hit repeatedly by 20mm and 37mm shells. Four RMs and two ORs from 30 CU were badly wounded. Despite the fierceness of the counter-attack, the ship's attack knocked out each of the enemy gun positions and large fires broke out in Monte Cuma, one being a huge blaze from a petrol dump. The LCI (L) then left at full speed to Ischia where they dropped off their wounded. This proved unsatisfactory because the hospital was alive with vermin, so the wounded were sent to Capri and transferred to a hospital ship.

30 CU was immobilized for a week after this attack as the LCI (L) was in bad shape and had to undergo a refit. This was particularly frustrating as reports come in of the enemy naval installations in the Naples area and the torpedo and midget submarine works around Baia, where they were keen to acquire intelligence.[1]

30 CU needed to acquire suitable craft for operations in the Bay of Naples. After several days were wasted trying to refit a former Yugoslav diesel craft, arrangements were made for the loan of another LCI (L). This wasn't as satisfactory as one would think as the vessel had several problems, one of which was the loss of a propeller. The vessel's top speed was 8 knots. This didn't persuade 30 CU to abandon any operations, however. They had learnt that the enemy was withdrawing and the amount of attacks on shipping was on the decline, therefore they would attempt a landing at Baia the next morning.

It was the evening of 23 September that the LCI (L) started its operation. Lieutenant Glanville was supported by Lieutenant Taylor and the newly instated Captain Coates. Their operation was most dangerous, being due to sweep past every known enemy position from Monte Cuma, through Monte Procida and Cape Miseno, into the Gulf of Baia. Not only that, the LCI (L) would spray these hot-spots with cannon-fire. The operation went smoothly. Alarm signals were released from many of the target areas but no return fire was given. On that basis a landing was planned for the following day. Two sections were planned to land at Baia, one by Captain Coates and one by Lieutenant Glanville. Coates planned to reconnoitre the enemy positions between Baia and Pozzuoli, and inland towards Lago D'Averno (with a view to capturing as much documentation as they could along the way). Glanville, however, was to examine the Baia torpedo works, to carry out countermeasures against any demolitions not completed and then to take a patrol inland to Licola. Both sections had their work cut out, with a difficult combination of activities and the high risk of encountering the enemy at close range.

The landing was made without enemy opposition, although considerable difficulties were caused by sunken wrecks. The SIC torpedo works were found to have been partially demolished. A number of charges and fuzes were removed and the plant placed under Italian guard with RM NCOs in charge. A preliminary survey revealed an interesting collection of experimental torpedoes and components as well as some Minisini-type midget submarines. A German torpedo depot was discovered nearby on Lake Lucrene. It had been demolished, although a quick search of the wreckage revealed a few papers of interest. Shortly after this search was completed a time bomb exploded in the foundations of the building.

At approximately midday Lieutenant Orton arrived, having travelled overland. He had accompanied the leading troops into Naples two days earlier and then pressed on ahead in his truck with three RM ORs. They were accompanied by some Italian partisans with whom they had fought during the liberation of Naples. Orton explained that he had not paused to search intelligence targets on the way through, as the shipyards at Castellammare and the factories in the southern suburbs, as well as the port area, had been severely damaged both by Allied bombing and the German demolition parties. In these circumstances, he pressed on to join up in the Baia area with the party operating from Ischia with whom he had arranged a rendezvous.

The evening of 23 September, Lieutenant Orton had established an advanced headquarters in a house at Posilipo. The next morning he had set out across the Campi Flegrei and, aided by his Italian partisan guides, had succeeded in reaching Baia shortly after noon. He had, in doing so, crossed the enemy lines at two points and had come under fire from LMGs near Lago D'Averno. The party suffered no casualties and Orton was able to observe the location of several enemy defence posts, and also to establish that the Germans were withdrawing towards the Volturno River, through Monte Cuma, Licola and Lago Di Patria.

Captain Coutes explored the area around Monte Nuovo to check enemy positions, while Lieutenant Glanville, with the partisan guides, attempted to reach Licola. Their aim: to try and capture the radar and communications centre.

Captain Coutes succeeded in finding the advanced battalion headquarters and captured some very valuable material, including annotated maps showing the location of all German units in the area. This was immediately sent back to the SCI at Capri for transmission to X Corps, where it was well received.

Glanville and his team managed to reach Monte Cuma, where the arrival of the party almost coincided with the withdrawal of the Germans. A detailed search was made of the whole area, including the Sybilline caves, as well as a number of farm buildings used by the Germans and local headquarters. Some papers of extreme value were discovered, including a complete set of the AHM from 1 January 1942 to date. The Germans were observed in some strength on the road towards Licola. When the search of the area had been completed, the party withdrew and reached Baia without incident.

The next day these incidents were repeated, Captain Coates continuing to explore the area between Baia and Bagnoli, while Lieutenant Glanville, with five ORs and two Italian partisans, set out for Licola. On this occasion the enemy were observed in about company strength in the village. The partisans volunteered to find their way into the centre in order to spread rumours that some 600 British troops had landed and were approaching. This scheme proved most effective, as the Germans immediately fired charges under the lock and pumping machinery and then escaped towards Lago Di Patria,[2] demolishing several bridges and culverts behind them.

The party made their way into the radar and communication centre. This was found to consist of an extensive area of the sand dunes which had been fenced off with complicated patterns of barbed-wire entanglements, defended by fields of mines, both AP and AT. The house of the lock-keeper had been used as an office and headquarters building.

A search of this building revealed that all the CBs and other documents belonging to the station had been stuffed into a central heating furnace and fired. Fortunately, the fire had choked and the books were only charred at the edges. These documents proved to be of extreme value. A search of the whole enclosure revealed that all the electronic equipment had been removed intact.

Captain Coates had covered most of the Campi Flegrei in his search and had picked up a number of papers of military and security interest. The party returned to Ischia in the evening without incident.

Captain Hargreaves-Heap now returned from Sicily with the remainder of headquarters staff. With the extra manpower thus available it was decided to spend the next few days in clearing up the Naples area before much damage could be done to intelligence material by Allied occupation forces or civilian looters. The following general plan was made:

1. Intelligence material on Ischia itself, consisting of a radar jamming set, a giant Wurzburg and a Freya (both badly damaged) and a Wassermann girder type tower (in course of erection) was left under a guard of US Airborne troops. A signal describing this material had been sent to COIS Med.

2. To arrange a team to search Pontian islands, particularly Ventottene.
3. To search all the targets remaining in that area.

The following day, 26 September, Lieutenant Glanville and Captain Coates, with ten ORs, sailed for Ventottene in an Italian fishing boat. Some useful radar equipment was picked up on the island as well as some documents. Nothing of naval interest was found on the neighbouring islands.

By now it was considered safe for the underwater weapons specialists to make a detailed examination of the whole complex of torpedo targets around Baia. An escort of commandos under Corporal Shermuly GM was accordingly arranged and Messrs Taylor and Austin spent the next week in making a meticulous investigation into all the various activities of SIC and the German torpedo depot. A representative collection of material and related documents was selected for shipment to the UK. These papers proved to be of considerable value.

The remainder of the Ischia party were now occupied with salvaging items of value from the wreckage of the big industrial plants along the north side of the Bay of Naples, which had been severely damaged by German demolitions and the various Armed Forces targets which still remained to be covered. The principal objectives so dealt with were:

1. The Ansaldo (ex Armstrong) Armaments Works at Pozzuoli.
2. The ILVA Steelyard at Bagnara.
3. The seaplane base at Nisida.
4. The shipyard at Catellammare Stabia.
5. A number of minor industrial targets at Miseno.

The Ansaldo works yielded a comparatively rich harvest. The charges that had been placed under the heavy machines had failed to do much damage and, as a consequence, the drawing and technical offices had remained substantially intact. Of a number of valuable documents recovered, the following are worth mentioning:

1. Working drawings of the proposed Italian 90mm dual-purpose AA and AT gun.
2. A file of papers relating to the exchange of raw materials and manufacturing processes between Italy and Germany, including a series of explanations given by the Germans for the non-delivery of certain commodities to Italy.

These papers were removed at once to Ischia where they were further screened and sorted by Messrs Austin and Taylor, and then packed for shipment to the Admiralty.

The ILVA steelyard proved to be disappointing since the plant had been concerned solely in the production of low-grade standard steels from pig iron (from blast furnaces in the yard) and the smelting of scrap. A few interesting papers relating to air-raid damage and production figures for the war years were recovered. Otherwise the only feature of interest was the limited scope of the damage caused by German demolition charges that had been placed under heavy machinery and under the foundations of the blast furnaces.

The seaplane base at Nisda was taken in good condition and handed over almost immediately to a party of RAF technicians. The RAF was not then in a position to provide adequate guards and much valuable material was lost through looting by Italian civilians.

The shipyards at Castellammare were handled by a team under Captain Hargreaves-Heap. Some working drawings were recovered, including those relating to the construction, including the machinery, of a Regolo class cruiser, *Giulio Germanico*, and of a German-designed tank landing craft. These papers were duly shipped to Malta for transmission to the UK. Unfortunately they did not reach the Admiralty.

The industrial plants at Miseno yielded some documents of general interest. The underwater weapons specialists also visited the airfield at Battipaglia, where novel accessories for aircraft torpedoes were recovered.

A final search of the area did not prove very profitable. The only targets of particular interest being the Research Institute of the Consiglio Nazionale Delle Ricerche: Instituto Nationale Dei Motori. This institution, which had been carrying out certain research was investigated by Mr Taylor of DSR, who eventually published an interesting paper on the subject. The industrial targets in the port area of Naples were not dealt with as the damage from aid raids and demolitions was considered too extensive for any material to have survived. It was also doubtful whether these plants, apart from the Stabilimento Pattisin, were likely to yield anything of naval concern.

A final survey of the district, including the seaplane base at Lago Di Patria, was made by two teams under Captains Hargreaves-Heap and Coates, but nothing of any particular value was recovered.

It is clear that by this time 30 CU had found their stride, working with Americans and Italians, their own specialists and an increased task force. But it was not time to become complacent. More challenges awaited them.

Chapter 14

Continuing the Good Work

'The radio sets hauled into France by the agents for the British Special Operations Executive during the Second World War were a nightmare by modern standards. Occupying a suitcase, they needed an aerial strung for yards up a drainpipe, had cumbersome valves the size of light bulbs and could only transmit messages on a Morse sender. This kept the operator tapping for ages, while German detector units could triangulate on the source and close in.'

The Fist of God, Frederick Forsyth

It is an obvious fact, but one worth mentioning, that the intelligence, blueprints and equipment that 30 CU acquired throughout was highly prized and important in its day – even ahead of its time – in certain instances, but by today's standards – sixty years later – almost prehistoric. This does not cheapen their contribution to the war effort, but it is a sad fact that most technological advances are made during times of war – as we will see in a later chapter – and 30 CU felt, because they were at the cutting edge of the front line, that they were in a race against time to capture enemy intelligence, to stop the building of more sophisticated machines and headquarters, and counter what was already substantive.

Although scientists were brought into the work at the Bay of Naples, they were mostly completing investigation in Sicily and the south of Italy, where there was less fighting.

When the naval installations and stores at Trapani, and on the Messina peninsula, had been cleared up, Lieutenant Commander Lincoln and Lieutenant Ogle travelled by sea to Salerno, but arrived at a time when the military situation there was critical, and when there was no likelihood of Naples falling in the immediate future. They therefore re-embarked and made their way to Taranto.

This port had fallen on 9 September, following a combined assault by seaborne and airborne forces. Unfortunately, the Officer Commanding 30 CU had had no notice of this operation and consequently the unit was not represented in the early stages. It is probable that valuable documentation was lost as a consequence. The specialist officers, on the other hand, discovered a quantity of material of extreme value in Taranto harbour, including the only specimen so far recovered of the German KKG Acoustic (Explosive) Sweep. This discovery led to modifications in the Royal Navy mining practice – a real tangible victory for the unit.

After Taranto had been cleared up, Messrs Austin and Taylor went to Naples. They continued up to Termoli, searching all ports and installations on the way. These operations yielded a modest return in documents and material relating to underwater weapons. Unfortunately, the manpower of the unit at this period did not allow for all the targets in the south of Italy being searched, let alone captured. It is possible that some of these objectives, particularly the radar and communications centres, might have yielded valuable intelligence material.

While all this was going on Lieutenant Commander Riley had been planning future operations in the Mediterranean and the shipment of documents and equipment captured. On 24 September, he left Salerno for Malta, arriving on the 26th. Here he attended a series of meetings with COIS Mediterranean and his staff, to whom the following proposals were sent:

1. That an advanced base be set up on one of the Dalmation islands in order to make contact with the guerrilla forces

operating in Yugoslavia, with a view to securing their participation in raids on German objectives in the Adriatic.

2. That a headquarters be installed at Bari or Brindisi to act as a base for any operations which might be mounted in the Adriactic.

3. That subject to the approval of FOWIT and other authorities concerned, a similar party to that mentioned in proposal 1 (above), should be sent to Corsica in order to participate in small-scale raids on the coasts of Italy and southern France.

COIS agreed to these proposals and gave Riley directions as to current Admiralty requirements. Riley proceeded to Brindisi where he reported to the NOIC and also made contact with Commander A. Wellman RN, the Officer Commanding Coastal Forces in the Adriatic, with his headquarters in the Coastal Forces Depot Ship, HMS *Vienna*.

The general situation in the Adriatic was discussed at a meeting attended by Commander Wellman, Lieutenant Commander Riley and Lieutenant Commander Bajkoff, of the Royal Yugoslav Navy, who had just escaped from Split. It was decided that an effective control of the Adriatic had to be exercised. A party had to be deployed quite swiftly to hold Viz. The political situation on the Dalmation islands was not clear. It was established that the Italians had withdrawn their forces from Yugoslavia at the time of the capitulation and that Yugoslav forces, described as 'Partisans' or 'Chetniks', had taken over the administration of the areas so evacuated. But the name and location of the authority to whom these people owed allegiance, and also the question as to whether the Germans had in fact succeeded already in reconquering the key points in the newly liberated territory, were as yet unknown outside certain narrow circles.

Later Riley made contact with a number of other Yugoslav refugees holding varying shades of political opinion, and from them he was able to draw up some sort of picture of conditions on the mainland. At the same time he sent Lieutenant Glanville, who spoke Serbo-Croat, to come from Ischia.

When Glanville arrived, a meeting was held on board HMS *Vienna* to draw up plans for operations in the Adriatic. It was agreed that the most important target for 30 CU was the Silurificio Whitehead at Fiume, where, according to the assistants of Admiral Minisini at Baia, the Germans had been conducting tests with new and experimental types of torpedo. In addition to this, the following objectives were selected as being suitable for 30 CU:

1. The radar at the communications centre at Lokri, off Dubrovnik.
2. The shipyard at Split.
3. The Naval and Naval-Air headquarters at Sibenik.
4. The German military headquarters at Dubrovnik and Metkovic.

On 16 October, Lieutenant Comander Riley, Lieutenant Glanville and six RM ORs, sailed for Vis in two MTBs under the command of Commander Wellman. The boats were fired upon as they approached Vis harbour, but once the party was ashore the nature of the missions was explained to the town commandant, a youth with a somewhat chequered career in relation to collaboration with the Axis occupying forces. A conference was accordingly held with the local Partisan authorities, who guardedly admitted that they were in the country military missions from England and Russia. They stated that they did not know how to get in touch with these missions, nor where they were located. 30 CU's field team was therefore requested to remain on Vis until their proposals for operations on the Dalmation coast had been submitted to Partisan headquarters. Riley returned to Bari.

Two days later Lieutenant Commander A.R. Glen RNVR arrived in Vis bearing a message from Riley ordering him and Lieutenant Glanville to meet with Brigadier F. Maclean, Head of the British Military Mission to the Yugoslav Partisan Forces, who was reported to be at Korcula on the island of that name. It was decided that representatives of all the British organizations on

Vis should proceed to Korcula and report their presence to Brigadier Maclean.

On 21 October (Trafalgar Day), Lieutenant Commander Glen, Lieutenant Glanville and Captain J.E.D. Evans of MI6 informed Partisan headquarters at Vis that they proposed to sail that night for Korcula in order to contact the British Military Mission. This proposal met with a good deal of obstruction on the part of the Yugoslavs, who claimed that the Brigadier was not on Korcula and they didn't want to sail anyway because of the threat of meeting German forces. It was pointed out that the object of the MTBs presence was to find the Germans and that the party would sail straight away. After some discussion the MTB, led by Lt D Scott RN, arrived at Viliki Otok on Korcula soon after midnight.

The Partisans here proved much more amenable and provided a truck to carry the party to Korcula, which was reached at 0330hrs. When Brigadier Maclean expressed some indignation that unauthorized persons should have entered his territory without referring to him, it was explained that until twenty-four hours previously not one of those concerned had been aware of the whereabouts of the Mission or of Brigadier Maclean's position as its head.

30 CU plans were explained to the Brigadier, who agreed that the case should be submitted to Marshal Tito to secure his consent for the co-operation of the Partisans in raids for certain objectives. He also agreed that Lieutenant Glanville should cross to the mainland and proceed to Marshal Tito's headquarters in order to explain the requirements of 30 CU and to endeavour to arrange for the collaboration of the Partisan forces. Meanwhile, the section of RMs was to transfer to Hvar, where the headquarters of the Navy section of the Mission was situated. Here, soon after arrival, an enemy craft with escorts was sighted sailing towards Brac. They succeeded in making Split, as the RN MTBs were short of fuel and the Yugoslav batteries did not open fire. It is possible that they were carrying some valuable documents.

Glanville, accompanied by Marine Plaxton and a Yugoslav

guide, sailed from Hvar and landed at Podgora. They then hitch-hiked inland to Livno in Bosnia, which was the local Partisan Army Headquarters. They then started by road for Jajce (Tito's headquarters), but met Brigadier Maclean at Bugojno (who had flown to Jajce). He informed Glanville that Marshal Tito was requested to return to Italy as soon as possible.

The whole party returned to Livno and in due course returned to Bari by way of Hvar and Vis. It was stated that Glanville was unacceptable to Tito and later accusations were made that Glanville had interfered in local politics and made a public speech in favour of General Mihailovic. These stories were quite unfounded and were probably the creation of the Partisan Security Service (OZNA), since Glanville's activities in Yugoslavia at the beginning of the war would suggest to the OZNA that he belonged to the 'Intelligence Service' and was likely to inquire deeply into local affairs.

It was unfortunate that these negotiations with Tito were not successful, since the Silverificio Whitehead undoubtedly held documents and material of extreme value. It transpired later that the German technician who was conducting experiments there at this time was none other than Dr Schubert of the TVA. He was killed by the Partisans in July 1944 and was therefore not subjected to interrogation.

Lieutenant Glanville's falling out with Tito could not have been foreseen. The correct procedure would have been for Lieutenant Commander Riley to have submitted his proposals to MO4 in Cairo for them to arrange the necessary clearance. The principal reason why this course was not followed was that at this time the unit had no permanent liaison with the high-level planning staffs in the Mediterranean and were consequently not aware of the function of MO4. The task in question would normally have fallen to Lieutenant Philips in Cairo but he was then heavily engaged in operations in the Aegean (see Chapter 15). It is doubtful if MO4 could have handled negotiations as they knew little about 30 CU and their primary function.

The lessons learnt from this more political episode were: that it was necessary for an Intelligence Assault Unit to maintain liaison with all the high military authorities in the area in which it happened to be operating; and that where operations involved collaboration with organizations holding extreme political views, such as the Yugoslav Partisans, it was essential that the antecedents of every officer directly involved should be analysed to avoid Glanville's situation.

'I complacently remembered that I had always "Demanded the impossible", that I had "Dared extreme occasion", and that I had "Not taken counsel of my fears".'

War As I Knew It, General George S. Patton

Chapter 15

Concluding the Mediterranean

'Despite the friendships I have made since the war, it is always those early ones that have weight, understanding, confidence and mutual experience that I cling to.'

'Rommel?' 'Gunner Who?' – A Confrontation in the Desert,
Spike Milligan

To conclude the first part of this history and ostensibly the first year of 30 CU's existence, I now need to detail the unit's operations in the Aegean. After this, the unit returned to London and began preparations for Operation OVERLORD, which starts the second part of this history.

This book is split into two parts because: a) it was important to detail the unit's first year meticulously, to highlight the lessons learnt and show where the influence for certain areas of its growth came from; and b) once the unit was part of OVERLORD, it was quite established and part of a much bigger and intricate project. It is the vastness of this bigger project – the invasion of Europe and the covert V1 and V2 work – that also dictated the break-up of this history. Although there are documents in the National Archive that outline the detail of 30 CU's first year, there are none that do the same for OVERLORD and beyond. The return to London – as mentioned at the end of this chapter – is the point where 30 CU transformed from a Secret unit to a Top Secret unit, so that the research that I have had to collate for this second part was far more disparate and is primarily where I had to check certain incidents with veterans for clarity. But before 30 CU's return to London, let us return to the Aegean.

It had been Lieutenant Commander Riley's original intention for the Army Troop to operate in the eastern Mediterranean as a self-contained unit. His clear idea was to have Captain Ward in command, with Lieutenant Philips in support and then Staff Officer (Intelligence) Levant. In view of the shortage of shipping available for the passage from Algiers to Alexandria, it was decided that the section under Captain Martin-Smith should gain operational experience in the Sicilian campaign and proceed afterwards.

On 5 July 1943, Philips and Ward flew to Cairo and, during the next three or four days, made themselves known to the officers directing the local branches of the clandestine organizations and to MO3 and MO4, and also reported to Commander Armstrong RN, the SO at RNHQ. On the 11th, the two officers travelled to Alexandria where they met certain members of the staff of Staff Officer Levant, as well as COIS and SO (P). All these contacts were made smoothly and the officers concerned proved most helpful and co-operative. This can be attributed in a large measure to the personal letter addressed by CCO to the various authorities in question, requesting that they give all possible assistance to 30 CU. This letter was received in good time and duly circulated, with the satisfactory results described.

The first problem to be solved was that of finding accommodation for the troop during their periods of waiting for operations. Eventually, after a number of alternatives had been considered, permission was obtained to use the Ski School in the Lebanon for this purpose.

On 24 July, Captain Ward returned to Algiers in order to bring his men from Bone, where they had encamped, to their new quarters. Lieutenant Philips first confirmed the arrangement for taking over the Ski School and then, early in August, proceeded to Sicily to report to Lieutenant Commander Riley. Here he was joined by Ward, who had travelled via Algiers. The position in regard to the disposition of the Army Troop was discussed at a series of meetings and it was finally decided that the section under Captain Martin-Smith should remain in the Italian theatre, leaving Captain Belcher and his team to handle targets in the Lebanon.

In due course, Philips and Belcher proceeded with their men to the Lebanon. A number of small-scale operations were discussed with special Raiding Forces (SRF) Aegean, but nothing materialized until after the capitulation of Italy, when it was decided by High Command Middle East to send forces to take over certain of the Aegean islands. A lift was accordingly requested and obtained for a Naval Advanced Intelligence Party, accompanied by a section of 30 CU, to reconnoitre the islands and handle any intelligence targets which might be encountered.

A special party was fitted out by Staff Officer Levant and consisted of Lieutenant Comander W. Croxton RNVR in command, Lieutenant M. Soloman RNVR, Lieutenant Philips, Captain Belcher and seven ORs of 30 CU (Army Troop). This team sailed for Leros in HMS *Fury*, arriving on 22 September.

The occupying forces consisting of a brigade reinforced by a detachment of SRF. They were under the command of Major General Brettorius, who set up his headquarters in Portolago. Force 292 (SOE) was established in a private house about 200 yards from Brigade, while the RN party was allotted a suite of six rooms at Brigade Headquarters to serve RNHQ. No accommodation was found for the Navy staff until the NOIC; Commander Villiers RN, succeeded in installing the RN party and 30 CU in the Italian Naval Barracks, which was situated on the opposite side of the harbour, some 5 miles distant by road.

The Italian Naval authorities received the party without enthusiasm. The impression gained was that the Italians were hedging their bets and were neither co-operative nor obstructive – just a pain in the rear end!

On 24 September, Lieutenant Commander Croxton returned to Alexandria to report; and a party consisting of Lieutenant Soloman in command, Captain Belcher and six ORs of 30 CU (one private being sick) carried out a reconnaissance of the island of Naxos. That afternoon a report was received that a large enemy merchantman was aground off the western tip of the island of Icaria. It was decided to attack it. In spite of a thorough search no enemy ship was sighted, so the boats returned to harbour.

Lieutenant Soloman's party had sailed at 1515hrs on the 24th, and at 0415hrs next day they made fast against the rocks at Eskinosa, covering two boats with camouflage netting and greenery. This work was completed in good time, since within two hours a low-flying JU 88 passed overhead. No Germans or Italians were found on the island and, leaving the boats behind, the party, now strengthened by the addition of Lieutenant Macleod RNVR with a Greek and an Italian liaison officer, sailed at 1120hrs in two small coastal boats, arriving at 1335hrs in Kalandos Bay, Naxos. The Italian lookout post had been demolished, the Italians having left on the 22nd, when two German schooners with an E-boat and a motor launch had entered Naxos Bay and landed troops, who had taken up defensive positions in the hills, based on Calchi.

At 1500hrs the party set out across the hills, both on foot and on mules. They were guided over some 20 miles of extremely rough track by Greek partisans, arriving at Filoti at 2030hrs. Here Soloman held a conference with the Greek and Italian authorities.

Next morning the party proceeded to Calchi for a similar meeting and at 1530hrs left Calchi for Naxos by Italian transport. At Naxos, Lieutenant Macleod read the official Allied proclamation to the people of the island. Later, at 1740hrs, they were in time to prevent an Italian, Lieutenant Duchi, from escaping from the island. This officer had been sent by the Germans at Syra to rally Naxos and Paros to the Axis cause.

The day after, the party went to the village of Pyranthos where a violent anti-Italian demonstration was calmed by Captain Belcher and his men. At 1700hrs they returned to Naxos and at 2130hrs went on board, sailing for Paros at 0300hrs next morning, the 28th, taking with them Duchi and a German Flight Sergeant who had made a forced landing at Kufronisi.

The boats stood off Paros harbour at 0600hrs while Captain

Belcher and Lieutenant Macleod, with an NCO, carried out a reconnaissance of the harbour. They signalled in due course that the way was clear for a landing. After ascertaining the general situation in relation to the Greek civil population and the Italian occupying forces, the party sailed for Leros, arriving at 0800hrs on the 29th.

The reconnaissance of the island was regarded more as an exercise than an operation. Nevertheless valuable intelligence was gained as to the general military and political situation on the island visited, and on the basis of the investigations and interrogations carried out, Lieutenant Soloman prepared a report to Staff Officer Levant, which proved to be of considerable value.

Captain Belcher, Soloman and seven ORs of 30 CU sailed on the evening of the 29th for Kalimnos, where the new headquarters of SRF had been set up. Here they remained for about five days. During that time they didn't deal with any intelligence targets or raids.

After the successful invasion by the Germans of Kos on 3 October, it was decided to withdraw the SRF from Kolimnos and they arrived at Portolago (Leros) early on the 4th. They were busy on the quayside, assembling their kit and equipment, when a heavy German dive-bombing attack took place, direct hits being obtained on the quay and its surroundings. Captain Belcher and Privates Ashton and McDavid were killed instantly. Staff Sergeant Wilkinson and Corporal Bancroft were severely wounded, the latter dying in hospital a few hours later. Private Maclennan was also slightly wounded.

The military situation on Leros had grown desperate. Air raids had been taking place daily. The Italian AA defences, at any rate in the early stages, had not opened fire and HMS *Intrepid* and HMS *Queen Olga* had been sunk. Military objectives were being bombed systematically. It was stated by the Italian ORs that the majority of their officers held fascist sympathies and it would appear that all movements were reported to the Germans via clandestine channels.

When the news of the evacuation of Kos was received, Italian morale collapsed and all sense of law and order vanished; 4, 5 and 6 October were given over to the looting of all the stores and dumps on the island. A further result of the breakdown in the organization was a general shortage of labour, which caused serious difficulties in the unloading and transport of stores and supplies.

A number of changes were made in the dispositions of the Allied command. With the object of avoiding attacks from the air, the Brigade had moved to a new headquarters up the hill. The Italian command had established itself in the underground operations room in the WT station at Portolago. NOIC moved to a small house near Brigade where the survivors of 30 CU followed on 5 October. The new headquarters were bombed again on the 5th and 6th. On the 7th the General moved his battle headquarters to Monte Meraviglia.

Lieutenant Commander Croxton arrived from Budrum, where he had been supervising the evacuation of the wounded from Kos. Plans were made immediately for the stretcher case (including Staff Sergeant Wilkinson, whose leg had been amputated) to be transported to Budrum. Three wounded men, accompanied by a doctor, Lieutenant Commander Croxton and Lieutenant Philips, accordingly sailed for Budrum where they arrived early on the 8th, eventually making their way back to Alexandria by way of Syria.

The survivors of the Army Troop joined up with SRF under Lieutenant Colonel Lord Jellicoe. They fought with distinction during the German invasion and were commended for their gallantry, Private Levy being appointed King's Corporal on the field. The three survivors returned with the SRF at the time of the final evacuation of the island.

Apart from Lieutenant Soloman's report on the political military situation on the islands, these operations paid no dividend whatever and resulted in relatively heavy loses. In fact 30 CUs participation appears to have been mishandled almost from the start. The principal criticisms made were:

1. When the operation was planned there were no intelligence

targets on the island for 30 CU. If they were deployed, they should have devoted their time to uncovering targets of opportunity. Instead they were relegated to reconnaissance work or to guard duties with the SRF.

2. Lt Philips allowed himself to be detached from the unit for liaison duties with the Italians. Admittedly he was only acting in accordance with orders received from the local NOIC but it was felt that he should have explained the nature of his appointment and his responsibilities to the unit, and obtained his relief from liaison work or kept it to an absolute minimum. There was a general tendency on the part of senior naval officers to propose to make use of the officers of 30 CU as interpreters or liaison officers. It was generally found that if the nature of the unit's operations was explained, the situation was rectified without any difficulty.

3. No adequate arrangements appear to have been made for the administration of the Army Troop, particularly in the event of casualties to their officers. As an Army unit operating under the RN their position was anomalous and although they were attached nominally to the SRF, they do not appear to have been properly provided for when the operation was originally planned.

It was clear that 30 CU had been misused and their remit not appreciated – the officers of the unit should have made their position very clear, but failed. The Admiralty – especially Commander Fleming – was furious. He hated the idea of his 30 CU being used as a run-of-the-mill commando unit, and now lives had been lost.

Fleming had lost his original DNI, John Godfrey, back in December 1942 and Commodore Rushbrooke had taken over the mantle. Technically, Fleming was a humble assistant to the DNI again and had to argue his cause properly through DNI, who was sympathetic overall.[1] What was his remit? Bring them home and regroup as their modus operandi had been severely shot through. But there was one big problem: 30 CU were reporting to COHQ, not directly to the Admiralty. Perhaps now the unit had fallen into disrepute they should come home to NID and report to DNI – what Fleming recommended. Nobody really wanted to be tarred with the 30 CU brush – it was almost as if they were in disgrace, although they weren't; but they had upset people.

Fleming wanted them back before anything else could go wrong, and he was given a large hand in this as he had Lieutenant Commander Riley's report – and lessons learnt – that made very sober reading. It explained that there were not enough men in theatre and more should be supplied. After such a cock-up, this was akin to shooting oneself in the foot, more so when Captains Ward and Huntingdon-Whitely travelled to London with Lieutenant Commander Curtis, Sergeant Kruthofer and other NCOs in order to train recruits! This knocked everyone sideways because they had reported back without obtaining permission from C-in-C Mediterranean to leave the area.[2]

DNI also considered that in any case the detachment, at one time of so many experienced officers and men, was an error of judgement and jeopardized current operations in theatre. Also, it was up to DNI to decide whether an increase in effort was necessary and to secure the concurrences of other authorities concerned (who 30 CU had upset quite considerably along the way). Furthermore, the conduct of the underwater weapons specialists was criticized because they removed equipment and documents from the area without obtaining the permission of COIS Mediterranean. It was also noted that arrangements for shipping equipment left on the quayside at Malta had been made in a very pompous and high-handed way. In short – and to use an old expression – they were in deep shit.

The men of the unit were tired and some were traumatized or physically scarred. To be told that they shouldn't have been deployed in such a manner was no good as an afterthought. This was a situation where lessons learnt didn't apply and friendships formed had been lost in the blood and dust. This was no melodrama and the Admiralty felt the same way – they weren't going to risk more men when the unit was being deployed by other powers to carry out operations outside their remit.

Despite their losses, the men on the ground were already regrouping. After the conclusion of the operations already described, the main field headquarters of the unit was established at Bari, with one section, drawn from the Army Troop, detached for duties in Corsica.

A villa near Bari was requisitioned by Captain Hargreaves-Heap and transformed into a headquarters and training centre. Seven and a half miles out of the main town at Torre A Marre, it proved to be the perfect location. The officers stationed there were: Captain Hargreaves-Heap, Lieutenant Commander Riley, Lieutenants Glanville, Orton, McFee and Philips, and Surgeon Lt H.R. Gray.[3]

News quickly got back from London and straight away all the specialist officers were called home. Not just Austin and Taylor but all the Admiralty underwater weapons specialists too.

Things were suddenly looking bleak and the wheels of change began to roll. Early in November, COIS Mediterranean, Captain Bousfield, paid a visit to the unit, and 30 CU quickly requested action in S Troop's capture of Rome, a parachute drop at Monterotondo to take a communications centre, a seaborne raid on a radar station at Marinella, and a parachute drop on the steel yard and armaments factory at Terni, with documents and material to be carried back through the lines on foot!

Captain Bousfield came to the following conclusions concerning 30 CUs proposals:

- Permission was granted for 30 CU to be represented in the S Force for Rome and Lieutenant Glanville was accordingly appointed to represent Naval interests on the Planning Staff.
- The raid on Monerotondo was agreed to in principle, although in the event it did not take place, since SOE was unable to arrange a lift.
- Permission for the mounting of the seaborne raid was withheld since it was considered that the value of the target

was not sufficiently high to justify casualties.
- The Terni operation was considered promising, since blueprints of value might be recovered. It was pointed out, however, that conditions in the Umbrian hills in mid-winter did not favour deep-level penetration and for that reason the operation was held to be impracticable.

One could say that 30 CU were being given a slight morale boast ahead of being sent home, but that could be a little too cynical, for the following reason: they were to be put back into S Force, albeit in a small way.

The next few weeks were accordingly spent by the planning staff in arranging for the unit's participation in S Force. The central authority for this operation was Major Cave, who readily agreed to 30 CU entering Rome ahead of the general advance, subject to all documents and material captured being cleared through a central authority. On this basis it was arranged that 30 CU should handle the Ministero Delia Marina, the Naval WT and Communication Centres. It was also suggested that they endeavour to capture certain key personnel, such as Senator Belluzzo, who were known to have been engaged on scientific, technical and operational research for the Italian Navy.

So all appeared well in-theatre, however London was still cross: after the return of the specialist officers and the Admiralty scientists it was concluded that the value of the material and documents was negligible considering what was potentially out there. The whole first year was thus summed up as one gigantic learning curve and that the unit would be stripped down and rebuilt for the mighty task of Operation OVERLORD: the invasion of Western Europe. That would be 30 CU's acid test.

30 CU was recalled to the UK for intensive training, after re-assessment, for Operation OVERLORD.

DNI further expressed the opinion that 30 CU's operations in the Mediterranean had exceeded expectations, which was a bit of a contradiction in terms, but understandable: they could have done better but under the circumstances they did extremely well (and with the loss of life, morale had to be kept up). DNI then requested Colonel R.R.B. Neville RM, who was about to make a tour of the Mediterranean, to investigate 30 CU's activities, to report on individual officers, and to make such recommendations as he thought fit for the reorganization and expansion of the unit.[4]

Neville arrived at Bari on 27 November having previously visited the eastern Mediterranean and Malta. He immediately interviewed Lieutenant Commander Riley and addressed the officers of the unit. It was explained that although 30 CU had justified its existence by the results of its operations, there had been considerable criticism of the manner in which these results had been obtained and of the general behaviour of the unit when off duty (and in certain respects, on duty too!). The complaints made included:

- Charges of lack of discipline, looting and misconduct on the part of certain ORs.
- Failure, by certain officers, to observe the rules of service procedure.
- Eccentricities of dress on the part of certain officers.
- Miscellaneous complaints on disparate subjects.

Reference has been made to RM ORs; but specifically their problems were sleeping on watch in the front line (at Salerno), and looting. It was a minority but it shouldn't have happened. Compounded with this was the great leniency in which officers dealt with these crimes – if they dealt with them at all. Neville observed that this was largely due to the peculiar constitution of 30 CU, whereby the Formation Commander was a Naval officer *nominally* in charge of RMs serving under the Army Act. The temporary CO of the RM wing was Captain Hargreaves-Heap. He was a detachment commander and his powers of awarding punishment were therefore quite limited. In these circumstances regular service discipline tended to be disregarded and there were even instances of senior NCOs taking the law into their own hands and physically assaulting offenders.

Much of these troubles could have been avoided by returning the worst offenders to their units. In fact one individual was so disposed of. The RM officers were loath to take this step as a general rule on account of the shortage of manpower in the unit and the difficulty of obtaining suitable replacements. Fundamentally, of course, the problem went back to the original selection and basic training of the men of the RM wing. It is significant that during the whole of the period under review not a single charge or complaint was brought against a member of the Army wing.

The next charge – that of failure on the part of the officers of the unit to observe the rules of service procedure, was well founded, although the individuals responsible were not always actually part of 30 CU. In certain instances, such as leaving or entering an area without referring to the C-in-C, the offences committed were due to thoughtlessness and were, to that extent, inexcusable. On the other hand it is only fair to state that in many cases the officers concerned were either attached to the unit temporarily or were not on the strength of 30 CU at all. For instance, on one occasion a signal that caused offence to C-in-C Mediterranean originated from NID. Otherwise such shortcomings can be attributed to the peculiar nature of the units operations and the fact that the officers of the RN and RM wings at this period were, with the exception of Captain Huntingdon-Whitely, all RNVR or HO Officers. Probably much trouble could have been avoided if a single RN officer had been on the strength. A most useful function could have been performed by a Lieutenant RN in charge of a small Headquarters staff to handle communications, planning and the disposal of captured documents and material.

Complaints regarding eccentricities of dress on the part of officers were justified, although in many instances the officer concerned had just arrived from the front, where he had probably been wearing the ordinary infantry uniform, and had had to report to a NOIC's office before he had time to change into a regular uniform. The difficulty was aggravated by the fact that the heavy baggage of the unit containing officers' spare uniforms was usually kept at Rear Headquarters, so that all ranks serving in advanced areas were frequently separated from their kit for considerable periods. Other cases of laxity or eccentricity in dress were less excusable. At least one instance occurred of an officer wearing a captured Italian sky-blue cape with an Alpine hat when off duty, and there were similar departures from regulation.

The question of dress was taken quite seriously; it was also noted some members of 30 CU wore Eighth Army uniform, which wasn't acceptable. It was also stressed that Admiralty scientists given temporary commissions as Naval officers should be properly briefed on Naval discipline, dress and deportment. The gentlemen who were attached to 30 CU at this time had received no such briefing and were consequently not instructed in the procedure to be followed when calling on senior officers and in general matters of deportment, such as dress and saluting.

Colonel Neville finally obtained permission for the whole of 30 CU, with the exception of the Army Troop, to proceed by air to the UK where they were to be reformed, reorganized and expanded for the part they were to play in Operation OVERLORD. It was further arranged that Lieutenants Glanville and Davies should leave ahead of the remainder of the unit in order to undergo a special course of training for operations in the Far East. The unit as a whole arrived in London between 20 and 25 December 1943, and were instantly sent on leave.

DNI and others within the Admiralty, including Commander Fleming, assessed the work of 30 CU, the pros, cons, lessons learnt and the findings – and conclusions – of Neville and reconstructed the unit for the New Year.

Part 2

30 Assault Unit

'All the folks are thieves, and think us fair game.'

Lord Nelson – written from HMS *St George* in Revel Bay to
Admiral Earl St Vincent, May 1801

Chapter 16

Planning for Operation OVERLORD

A long COS meeting at which we did our weekly review of the threat of the rocket or pilotless plane [V1].

Diary entry 4 January 1944, *War Diaries 1939-1945, Field Marshal Lord Alanbrooke*, Edited by Alex Danchev and Daniel Todman

Colonel Neville's report concerning 30 Commando was taken very seriously and resulted in a series of meetings at COHQ. His final recommendations were put forward and discussed with the first agreed action being the change of name from 30 Commando to 30 Assault Unit (30 AU). This proposal was put forward and agreed in December 1943.

Other proposed changes were not accepted – for example, Neville proposed the disbandment of the Navy element of the unit. DNI would not see his department's brainchild lose its soul (he was loyal to Fleming and his predecessor Godfrey). Also, the unit was born a Navy unit and a Navy unit it would stay (despite the so-called disgrace the RM element brought on the unit, which tarnished the RN side).

It was agreed that 30 AU would be split into two wings, RM and RN (the Army element to one side so no further criticism could be apportioned to them). The RN wing would be responsible for all intelligence and planning (under DNI) of the targets to be attacked. Also they would be responsible for the planning and handling of intelligence material in the field and, ostensibly, the disposal of documents and material captured.

The RM wing was to be responsible for all military planning, for the co-ordination and assessment of intelligence captured, for organizing the approach to objectives, their subsequent capture, and for guarding targets after capture. Furthermore, communications with outside authorities were to be handled by the RN wing (so DNI could keep an eye on things), while internal signals would be the responsibility of the RM.

It was also made clear that the unit would operate in the field under order of ACOS (I) to ANCXF, while the chain of command within each part of the unit would be Commander RNVR (for RN) and Lieutenant Colonel RM (for RM). And just to make a clean break of things, the main depot and Headquarters of the unit would move from Amersham to Littlehampton.

It came as a great surprise that Neville proposed that the Army Troop be disbanded too. Major General R.E. Laycock objected most strongly but was thrown a lifeline in the guise of Fifteen Army Group, who placed a high value on the services of 30 Commando and requested that the Army Troop should continue to serve on the Italian front. They were therefore reformed and proceeded to the Mediterranean under the name of the 'Special Engineering Unit of Commando Brigade'.[1]

The reorganization of the unit meant good news and bad for its members: at the request of SACSEA, Lieutenant Commander Riley was sent to organize an Intelligence Assault Unit in SEAC; Lieutenant Commander Curtis was promoted to Commander and placed in command of the RN wing with Lieutenant McFee promoted to Lieutenant Commander as second in command; Lieutenant Davies was retained for special duties in Corsica; Lieutenant Philips left the unit to become Liaison Officer to the French Navy at Algiers; Lieutenant Glanville was retained in Europe (because of his continental experience) and not to follow Lieutenant Commander Riley; Lieutenant Orton left the unit and became SO Sy Naples.

30 AU started life in the Admiralty Citadel[2] under the watchful gaze of their formation commander, Fleming. Additional

support would come from MI6 and, because of the sometimes delicate relationship between NID and MI6, DNI Commander Rushbrooke expected to be kept up to speed – by Fleming – on all aspects of the unit's planning and training. He demanded that adequate intelligence dossiers, including lists of targets and fully annotated maps, were to be prepared for each phase of a given operation.

Ever methodical and keen to ensure past mistakes didn't reoccur, Fleming proposed NID 30, an intelligence planning wing of 30 AU of which he would be head boy. NID 30 would have offices in the Admiralty and liaise with other departments within and outside the Admiralty, including MI6, SOE and Bletchley Park. DNI supported this idea fully but learnt very quickly that there weren't any spare staff to support this aspect of 30 AU, so it was agreed that the unit would support themselves. Certain Navy officers would be drafted in to the Admiralty to tackle the intelligence feed full time, with Commander Fleming's experience overseeing – but not interfering – as he was still DNI's personal assistant, and still had an important job to do there.

Simply because of the call of other work on Fleming, Commander Curtis became the head of section for NID 30 (attempts were made for Fleming and Curtis to split the work up but this became messy and lopsided). Lieutenant Glanville was requested to draft a document – a 'black list' – of Admiralty requirements in material and intelligence for the defeat of Germany. This would give greater structure to what 30 AU did in the field.[3]

Robert Harling from NID was attached to NID 30 to plot targets on maps and arrange printing.[4] Harling was a typographical consultant by profession and before the war had been an amateur yachtsman. He joined the RNVR in 1939 and served in escort vessels in the Atlantic. He took part in the evacuation at Dunkirk and was later drafted to ISTD, where he worked as a topographical and cartographical officer. He was now earmarked to assist 30 AU in the field too.

In January 1944, 30 AU was told to put its new staff and privileges to work and construct intelligence dossiers for each phase of Operation OVERLORD. In February they had constructed the following structure within the RN wing:

NID 30 – Structure of Duties

Commander Curtis: OC to RN wing and of the section. Mainly engaged on liaison duties with Army and US Forces.
Lieutenant Commander Postlewaite: liaison with DTM (I) in connection with torpedoes; otherwise engaged on topographic work.
Lieutenant Hugill: collaborating with Lieutenant Commander Postlewaite in preparation of target maps and geographical intelligence handbooks.
Lieutenant Ionides: liaison with DTM (I) in connection with mines; otherwise engaged on topographic work.
Lieutenant Commander Dalzel-Job: preparing target maps, etc. of Norway.

In Littlehampton

Lieutenant Commander McFee: in local charge of RN wing as 1st Lieutenant.
Lieutenant Besant: assisting McFee as administrator.
Lieutenant Van Cleef: Unit Signal Officer.
Sub Lieutenant Gray: Medical Officer to 30 AU.

The officers of 30 AU RN underwent the following training courses:
1. The unit as a whole took the long course at HMS *Volcano* in demolitions and counter-demolitions, the handling of explosives and enemy mines, bombs and booby traps.
2. The unit also took the full course at the London School of Street Fighting.
3. The officers of the Naval wing took special courses at Scotland Yard (directly across the road from the Admiralty), in the searching of persons and premises, care of prisoners, safe-breaking and lock-picking, and at the London Salvage Brigade in the recovery of material from damaged premises.

4. The officers of the Naval wing and, to a limited extent, the unit as a whole, were instructed in the recognition of enemy documents.

Members of 30 AU took other courses too, for example: Lieutenants Besant, Glanville and Hugill qualified as parachute jumpers at the PTS (Parachute Regiment), Ringway: Lieutenant Commander McFee and Lieutenant Long had already qualified while in North Africa; Lieutenant Commander Dalzel-Job managed to get his training in just before joining the unit; Lieutenant Ionides qualified as a diver; Lieutenant Besant took the course in photographic recognition at APIS, Medmenham; and Lieutenant Commander Dalzel-Job took the course in photography at the AFU, Denham.

30 AU veterans James Powell and Bill Thomas told the author in the spring of 2008, that the ORs in the unit took any course they could, because the extra qualifications meant more money and sometimes an OR would earn as much as an officer![5]

Members of 30 AU from Littlehampton were encouraged to drop in to NID 30 when on a course, and unit members at the Admiralty were encouraged to spend at least one day a week at Littlehampton.

Although the training was considered adequate, it lacked in some areas, primarily in the MI9 course in organizing escapes as prisoners of war and in behaviour under interrogation.

The organization and planning of the RM wing was less troublesome than previously experienced in the unit. Lieutenant Colonel Woolley RM was OC. His second in command was Major Hargreaves-Heap but was replaced by Major A.L. Evans RM, from the holding commando at Wrexham. Major Evans had qualified as a solicitor before the war and had a working knowledge of French.

Meanwhile the troop leaders, Captains Huntingdon-Whiteley, Douglas and Pike (commanding A, B and X Troops respectively), set about selecting men for the increased complements. The NCOs were largely drawn from the ORs who had served in the

Mediterranean. Otherwise RMs were inducted from the Holding Commando at Wrexham, from sea service and to a limited extent from the RM battalions. In the case of X Troop, selections were made with the ultimate objectives of the unit in view. Many of the men concerned had had police or other suitable experience, or else had knowledge of European languages.

As soon as the new complement was filled, the troops started a course of intensive training. The unit passed through the long course at HMS *Volcano* (in demolition and counter-demolition, the handling of explosives and enemy mines and booby traps), and the London School of Street Fighting. Normal commando training was also undertaken, such as speed marching, cliff climbing, night operations, amphibious warfare and demolitions, supplemented by special lessons in living on the countryside and life in the field.[6]

An Intelligence Section of the RM wing was instituted, comprising Lieutenant Bailey RM (who was fluent in German and Danish) and five ORs.

The unit came under the control of ANCXF on 1 May 1944 and from that date all orders relating to operations were issued by ACOS (I) to SNCXF.

It is interesting what 30 AU's remit was for Operation OVERLORD: documentation; intelligence concerning German torpedo design, mines and minesweepers; underwater obstructions in ports, harbours and naval installations; new types of radar equipment and search receivers, with particular reference to centimetre wave practice.

With all this in mind, two main objectives were selected for 30 AU:

1. The Naval HQ and the port area of Cherbourg.
2. The radio station at Douvres (to be captured by noon on D-Day).

Now primed, 30 AU were incorporated into Operation NEPTUNE in the following way: Pikeforce, consisting of X Troop (Captain Pike RM commanding) and Captain Hargreaves-

Heap, under Major Evans, with Lieutenant Glanville, one OR of the Intelligence Section and two SBAs were to land with the assault wave on D-Day at St Aubyn-sur-Mer, and then accompany the north shore regiment of Canadian Infantry inland and capture the Radar Station at Donres.

Lieutenant Commander Postlewaite and Lieutenant Hugill, with their drivers and RM orderlies, were to land at Arromanches on D-Day to search the radar station and then to join Commander Curtis to handle targets in the Ouistreham area.

Curtforce, with Commander Curtis in command, and with the Headquarters staff of the Naval wing, was to land at Port-en-Bessin, to search the lighthouse and lookout station and any vessels that might be lying in the harbour, and then to proceed to Ouistreham to carry out similar tasks and eventually to set up a unit Headquarters for the British area, at Douvres.

Woolforce, consisting of Lieutenant Colonel Woolley commanding, A Troop, B Troop, Captains Cunningham, Macgreggor and Lieutenant Long, were to land near Ste Mère Eglise on the Contentin Peninsular, and then accompany the US Task Force to Cherbourg to handle an agreed list of naval targets there.

Naval officers of the unit, with the exception of Lt Besant, who had been temporarily appointed to the staff of ACOS (I) to take care of 30 AU affairs, devoted the last two months before D-Day, in part, to an intensive study of the technical aspect of Intelligence requirements, and in part to military training and general fitting out, together with preparation for the operations in which they were to take part.

Transport and equipment for the RN wing had been secured by Lieutenant Commander McFee. This had presented a problem of some difficulty from an administrative point of view. Stores were secured by J.G. Ballantyne along with Lieutenantt Lambie USNR, who remained with the unit until the end of the operations in Europe. Other last-minute additions to the unit were Lieutenant Commander H.R. Ward RNVR and Lieutenant T. Tamplin RNVR.

Although the mechanics of the unit's preparations are

important, what of the individual? How did they prepare?
In his autobiography *Arctic Snow to Dust of Normandy* (Pen &
Sword, 2005), Patrick Dalzel-Job explained his daily routine after
moving from Littlehampton to the 'Cage' at Chichester:

> surrounded by barbed wire and cut off from all outside
> communication. Waiting for the weather to become suitable
> for the landings was irksome, but it was a physical holiday
> for me. I had done everything possible to maintain the good
> that had been done to me by the parachute course. I ran up to
> five miles every day before breakfast at Littlehampton,
> something which would have been no trouble for most men
> but into which I had to put a deal of effort.

Before D-Day members of 30 AU were all issued with special
passes, which 'by command of General Eisenhower' authorized
them to do practically anything anywhere, adding in block
capitals: 'THE BEARER OF THIS CARD WILL NOT BE
INTERFERED WITH IN THE PERFORMANCE OF HIS DUTY
BY THE MILITARY POLICE OR BY OTHER MILITARY
ORGANISATION.'[7]

30 AU knew almost everything about the plans for D-Day well
in advance, except the exact date, which, in fairness, was a
moveable feast because of the weather and several other factors.
Dalzel-Job mentioned in his autobiography that while walking
the corridors of the Admiralty he was told of the plans for
OVERLORD (and ostensibly NEPTUNE by another member of
staff who he didn't know – so much for being discreet).
However, by 25 May 1944, all preparations were complete and
the various detachments became ready to embark on Operation
NEPTUNE.

> 'Part of the unit was lucky enough to go ashore with the first
> British troops on D-Day, without loss, but the rest of us were to
> work on the American sector in the early stages. We landed
> near Varreville on "Utah" beach on 10 June (D+4).'
>
> *Arctic Snow to Dust of Normandy*, Patrick Dalzel-Job

Chapter 17

D-Day

The Normandy landing took place on 6 June 1944 and 30 AU were in the thick of it. Pikeforce landed first at Saint Aubyn-sur-Mer. The assault on this particular beach was led by 41RM and 48RM Commandos, who suffered heavy losses. 30 AU made it through into the village unscathed. Here they rendezvoused with the Canadian North Shore Regiment at the church at 1000hrs and they all set out towards Douvres.

They were on the Tailleville Road by noon but came under heavy mortar and machine-gun fire before reaching the chateau, which was being used as a German battalion headquarters. The battle lasted five hours but the chateau was eventually captured. Not only were some interesting documents taken from it, there was more information in the outhouses which had been used as a headquarters by the Gestapo.

The following day the unit progressed through the next village, but again progress was slow due to snipers in the buildings and trees. By nightfall 30 AU and their Canadian Allies were on the edge of the Tailleville Forest, which was also infested with snipers, but from the ridge they could see the radar station, which was their next objective.

By this time the Canadians had suffered heavy casualties and a meeting was held with 30 AU to discuss progress. A surprise attack was deemed to be a good idea but this was thwarted by the enemy. When the Canadian CO, Lieutenant Colonel Buele, reported his progress and heavy losses, he received an order from 3 Canadian Division relieving him from his task of capturing the defences at Douvres. This was good news as it was found that the enemy strength at Douvres was greater than thought. The survivors of Pikeforce and 4 Commando Brigade were assigned to 'contain and harass' the Germans in this region, although this didn't last long as Colonel Wooley pulled the unit out.

A 'rich harvest' was uncovered in the Douvres area, despite some looting, which 30 AU had to deal with. It was ascertained – much later – that Douvres had been the main communications centre as well as a radar station and the looting had been done by British troops (not attached to 30 AU). Professionally, Douvres was a pretty lousy performance.

The decision that 30 AU was not to participate in the assault had an unfortunate effect on the morale of the men; the unit was further criticized by Commando Group for a certain lack of enterprise in harassing the target. But this was just one section of 30 AU and the criticism was harsh.

Curtforce had set up camp in Crepon and were in good shape overall as they suffered no losses on landing at Asnelles-sur-Meron. Their first job on landing was taking the coast-watch radar station. This didn't provide too much of a problem because the radar station was empty, but there were enemy snipers in the area who posed a slight challenge to the unit. It appeared that the previous occupants had left in some haste as a car full of Top Secret documents was found parked outside and these proved to be of huge importance to the Admiralty.

Lieutenant Hugill made an investigation of the station at Pointe et Raz de la Percée. This proved to be a coast-watch station, with two giant Wurzburgs, one pole-type Freya and one coast watch. The area was also indicated by signposts as the 'ORTSKOMMANDANTUR'. The station had been heavily bombed from the air and shelled from land. Also, the scuttling charges had been blown under each of the sets. Although the operations hut had been destroyed, some useful manuals of instruction graded Geheime Kommandosache (Top Secret) were recovered.

RAF Flight Lieutenants Fishwick and Palmer joined Lieutenant Glanville to analyse German radar sets captured there. This proved to be difficult with all the hustle and bustle in the area, but the introduction of specialists was important to the logistics of sorting and prioritizing the equipment and documents recovered thus far.

All the documents and material recovered by 30 AU so far – including Douvres – were taken to the UK in instalments overseen by Lieutenants Hugill, Glanville and Lieutenant Commander Postlewaite. They were delivered to a store in Portsmouth dockyard, under the charge of Lieutenant Besant, where they were inspected by the interested Admiralty authorities, who had been notified by signal. Once this had been done, the 'loot' was distributed onwards to the people who could use the intelligence gained. This was proof, if proof be needed, that 30 AU were making a genuine contribution to the war effort.[1]

Documents and material recovered from the radar stations clarified all the problems with understanding German radar practice, such as the design and construction of magnetron valves and wave guides. One document found showed the location of every German radar station installed or projected in Europe, together with full technical particulars of the sets (including certain types of equipment which were not yet operational), and was 'assessed in the Admiralty as the greatest single technical capture of the war'. Other problems connected with the phasing gear for swinging the beam on fixed aerial arrays were cleared up at Douvres, which also yielded some valuable documents. It seemed that 30 AU were really getting hold of quality items now and their profile and importance was swelling. They had come of age.

From the point of view of radar, and to a lesser extent of documents relating to operational matters, these operations in the British zone of the NEPTUNE area were extremely successful. On the other hand, a number of targets of opportunity were missed, including such novelties as a dump of beach defence rockets and a light AA gun with a pendulum sight. The failure to discover these targets can probably be attributed to an excessive rigidity in planning, which allocated individual officers to specific targets without making any provision for those targets of opportunity which, in previous experiences of the unit, had generally yielded such rich results.

Chapter 18

V Rockets

'In a period of bad flying weather [18/19 June 1944], only 10 Mosquitoes could be sent to attack a large concrete flying-bomb storage building in the woods at Watten, near St-Omer. 9 aircraft bombed but no details of the results are available. No aircraft lost.'

The Bomber Command War Diaries, Martin Middlebrook and Chris Everitt

Woolforce landed at Utah at 1500hrs on D+4[1] and had moved into an assembly area at 2145hrs. The transport had not been landed, so the Americans were marched off. Lieutenant Colonel Woolley didn't want to be upstaged by the Americans so ran his men alongside to the astonishment of the Allies. The evening was warm and dark and Dalzel-Job was not happy with the additional exercise, stating in his autobiography: 'I think he [Woolley] would have done better to conserve our energy for what was to come.'

30 AU finally came to a halt in a field surrounded by hedges near Ste Mère Eglise. Only a few of the soldiers started digging in because no orders were given to do so. At 2320hrs a low-level bombing attack by about seven enemy aircraft, flying out of low cloud, resulted in AP bombs being dropped across the unit's encampment, causing severe casualties – both killed and wounded. Amongst the dead was Lieutenant Ionides. Captain Lamb and Sub Lieutenant Long were badly wounded.

Altogether five men were killed and sixteen wounded, out of a total of 190 in the unit.

In his autobiography, Patrick Dalzel-Job mentions this attack: 'Suddenly, there was an explosion like a bomb-blast immediately above us, followed by a peculiar fluttering noise in the air. For a while, nothing else happened; then the whole field was lit by sharp flashes and explosions, like heavy machine cannons firing sporadically around us.'

This was a dreadful error on 30 AU's behalf. They believed that they were sufficiently far enough away from the enemy to lay low for the night without taking normal – not extra – precautions. Dalzel-Job believed an officer should have given an order to cut trenches (or at least 'scrapes') to lie in for the night – which would have provided much protection for such an attack – but no such order was given. He explained the carnage in his autobiography:

Most of the men lying around us were wounded more or less seriously – nasty little holes in many cases, without very much outside bleeding. Doing what little I could for them by the light of a dismal torch, I was impressed and humbled again by the extraordinary stoicism and cheerfulness of wounded men. One, at least, of the many I bandaged was mortally wounded, as was a naval officer nearer the hedge [probably Lt Ionides].

The mental and physical scars the unit sustained from this incident were monumental and I would like to labour this point, just to bring to the reader's attention the unhealing scar of war. Here Dalzel-Job remembers the incident:

Death in war is often terrible, but Cpl Wright who died beside me did so quietly and without pain. A little while later, I passed an American soldier who had presumably been hit in the forehead by an explosive bullet. The top and inside of his head had vanished like the inside of a finished breakfast egg, but his face – like Cpl Wright's face – was quite calm in death.

The following day the transport was landed and the force moved forwards to Ste Mère Eglise itself, where Headquarters was set up. Lieutenant Colonel Woolley and Lieutenant Commander McFee made contact with Colonel King and Lieutenant Colonel O'Malley of VII US Corps, to establish orders. Original plans had to be recast in order to fit in with changes in the American order of advance. It was therefore decided that small teams should be sent out to investigate buildings which had been occupied by the Germans. During the four days 13-16 June, a considerable volume of papers of military interest were picked up in this manner and turned over to the US Army authorities. This is a very significant point, especially when the final arrest of top V rocket scientists occurred the following year (30 AU believed that they were largely responsible for these arrests while the glory went to the Americans).

On 17 June, the 'Ski' sites to the north of St Saveur le Vicomte were overrun. 'Ski' was the code name given to those monumental concrete emplacements which were constructed by the Germans, apparently to serve as bomb-proof stores for rocket missiles intended for the bombardment of the invasion coast. At the request of the Air Ministry these had become targets of the highest priority for 30 AU, and imperative to the countering of the V weapons offensive against southern England.

The Americans informed the unit that a gap had appeared in the German lines and it was possible to reach a V1 site of known location (at this time the RAF knew where most sites were and told 30 AU). Lieutenant Commander Dalzel-Job, with his right-hand man Bill Wright and another RM (possibly by the name of Paul McGrath), took Flight Lieutenant Nutting of ATI to the site.

Dalzel-Job remembered the day to be dry and warm as they made their way through the American line and into an area of fields and woods. They moved forward with care, keen to avoid snipers by crawling several miles across dry, dusty earth. Every now and then there was a burst of running but, all the time, the Troop was concerned about enemy attack. As was customary with commando units, the last man in the patrol had orders to turn round and beckon to a non-existent follower each time he came into open view, as there was evidence that this strategy worked – by causing a would-be assailant to hesitate before shooting, believing that more members of a patrol were following.

Dalzel-Job's troop then zigzagged across open ground, took exact compass cross-bearings from a combination of a church spire and a road junction, and reached the launch site in late afternoon. According to Dalzel-Job there were 'German equipment and belongings' scattered around, as if hurriedly abandoned. He didn't find anything he considered of particular interest to his 'untechnical mind', although 'the experts who were later guided to the site were very pleased, and especially as the first V1 flying bomb fell on London that day'.

The most difficult part of 30 AU's history to document is the significance and depth of their involvement in V-weapon countermeasures. Veterans from Woolforce claim that most of their time was taken up with this work and much was found (file ADM 223/214 in the National Archive claims that it was Woolforce's priority to counter V rockets and gather as much information as possible, but document very little – in fact, it says nothing was found). Also, veterans claim that 30 AU's Ralph Izzard was a guru on the subject of V weapons and that there were scientists attached to the unit who were specifically interested in this intelligence. Veterans also told me that much information concerning V weapons came from Commander Fleming as to the location of rocket sites. As mentioned before, the RAF knew where these sites were and the Air Ministry requested that Woolforce make V weapons their biggest priority, so clearly the Air Ministry fed the latest intelligence into NID and Fleming then fed it into Woolforce through the main American HQ (as 30 AU was attached to the American chain of command).

It is also stated by veterans that Fleming received intelligence from the French Resistance as well as the Air Ministry. This is interesting because it is known that a crashed British glider pilot by the name of Staff Sergeant Bramah worked with the Resistance and assisted Woolforce in Europe (see Dalzel-Job's autobiography). History dictates that the Americans arrested von Braun and other top Nazi V rocket scientists, which Woolforce believe they did, but not the Americans. It is clear to my mind concerning the latter point that the Americans took control of the scientists – thus creating Operation PAPERCLIP – through the chain of command Woolforce had to adhere to.

I believe it is very important at this juncture to provide a brief history of the air and ground European countermeasures against the V rockets that fell under the headings Operation CROSSBOW and Operation BIG BEN, to show for the first time where 30 AU, specifically Woolforce, fell into this mix. This will provide a sturdy framework for this very important part of 30 AU's history until the 100-year ruling on certain documentation expires and other information possibly comes to light.

'In those days, the great threat to London and to the south of England was believed to be Hitler's "Revenge Weapon No 1", the VI Flying Bomb.'

Arctic Snow to Dust of Norway, Patrick Dalzel-Job

On the night before the Normandy landings, Bomber Command flew 1,211 sorties, in support of the imminent landing. Strategically, forward bombing was essential to disorientate and destroy enemy units and command posts. But soon Bomber Command found itself diverted from such raids. The V1 rocket was launched against London six days after the landing and they were causing tremendous problems: widespread panic amongst civilians, homes and other building destroyed and, many, many lives being taken, mainly civilian. It would go down in history as the first full-blown terrorist attack on the civilian population of Great Britain. Bomber Command was ordered to destroy V1 sites, the first being in the Pas de Calais area. This caused frustration amongst the bomber crews because the V1 launch sites did not pose a threat to the invasion itself! For exactly one month Lancasters and Mosquitos bombed specific sites. Wing Commander Leonard Cheshire was ordered to leave 617 Squadron and rest on 6 July. He had flown both day and night flights against the V1 sites and two months into his rest, with an impressive total of four tours and 100 operations during his career, he was awarded the Victoria Cross. Cheshire was an important part of the airborne military response to the V1s, nicknamed Operation CROSSBOW, mainly because the sorties attacked the final enemy targets the Crossbow Committee (Churchill, Alanbrooke, Morrison, etc.) had been contemplating countermeasures for some time.

Aspects of Operation CROSSBOW were more daring than Operation BIG BEN. Spitfires dive-bombing was one thing, Lancasters doing it was another, as Russell Braddon wrote in his authorized biography of Cheshire, *Cheshire VC* (Evans Brothers Limited, 1954):

They flew off to the Pas de Calais. Flares were dropped from 12,000 feet. Then, as they had determined he should do in advance, privately and most illicitly, Martin had dived [his Lancaster] thunderously down to four hundred feet, having spotted the target, and had marked it perfectly... The bombers dropped their loads dead-on the markers and completely destroyed a huge rocket-launching site. It worked. But in a Lancaster it was a hair-raising business.

In his posthumous memoirs, *War As I Knew It* (The Riverside Press, 1947) General George Patton wrote that between 6 and 12 July 1944: 'The whole northern tip of the Cherbourg Peninsula was covered with launching sites for V1 bombs. These were very interesting.'

Patton didn't just make a cursory statement about these sites – spotted as soon as the invasion was successfully implemented – he went into some detail to explain what they were in his diary:

Usually a small concrete road, camouflaged to look like dirt, led off from a main road and eventually came to a concrete slab about the size of two tennis courts. On the edges of this slab were semicircular points where trucks could be left. Down the centre of the slab were a number of holes. At some of the sites were caves or dugouts in which rockets could be stored. In others these were absent. The method of procedure was that, during the night, a convoy containing a certain number of rockets and a knocked down ramp moved up. The ramp was erected by placing the uprights in the holes previously mentioned. It had an angle of about thirty degrees to the horizontal. The rocket was placed on this ramp, which had been carefully pointed to reach a certain area of England, and was then discharged.

Bomber Command hadn't made a good job of destroying the 'Ski' sites. This wasn't just the opinion of General Patton – 'Very few of the sites I visited had been successfully bombed' – it was the consensus of opinion at Fighter Command[2] and resulted in Spitfire squadrons being deployed from September to counter the V2 threat (Operation BIG BEN). 30 AU would become a major source of intelligence on the ground for Operation BIG BEN, starting with the information they found concerning V1s. Patton observed, again in his memoirs, that, 'When the supply of [V1] rockets was exhausted, the whole outfit [Nazis] picked up and left, while a detail remained to restore the camouflage.' This became an extremely important piece of intelligence for Dalzel-Job and his men and it came from the Americans to whom 30 AU were attached. They had located a site behind enemy lines and would make provision for 30 AU to go and capture important documentation and then return for their scientists to analyse the site more thoroughly. Incredibly and, according to Dalzel-Job's autobiography, this action took place the very day the first V1 fell on London: 12 June 1944.[3]

30 AU were deeply imbedded in Operation CROSSBOW (but very little is available to the public through the National Archive);[4] Commander Fleming would hear of their triumphs and in turn feed everything back to the Crossbow Committee through the proper sources. From here a clear and detailed

picture of the Vengeance threat could be grasped and countered.

Some very scary intelligence came back to London. Imagine hearing words like the following:

> There was another enormous construction, the reason for which has, so far as I know, never been explained. It consisted of a concrete block approximately a mile long and about sixty to eighty feet square. In the hills at either side, wedge-shaped excavations, approximately one hundred feet deep and two hundred feet wide at the top, had been made and filled with concrete. It is my opinion that there was more material in this construction than in the Great Pyramid.

These are the words of General Patton, at odds with a rocket hideout construction, the very establishments that 30 AU would explore, analyse and destroy, feeding every scrap of information back to London in a timely manner. But before the Spitfire squadrons could be made ready for Operation BIG BEN (specially made clipped-winged Mark XVIs, which were very quickly test flown), Mosquito squadrons were sent to destroy imminently dangerous sites. The bravery of the men who flew these sorties – basically a suicide mission – was captured so brilliantly in the movie *633 Squadron* (released in 1963, starring Cliff Robertson and George Chakiris); but largely ignored by historians since. And it was the Mosquitoes that appeased Patton's fears and bombed the large V rocket housing depots.

Although this book doesn't concern itself with the airside of Operation CROSSBOW, I wish to quote one sortie by Bomber Command (taken from *The Bomber Command War Diaries*, Martin Middlebrook and Chris Everitt) so that the intensity of the bombing is fully appreciated by the reader:

> [24/25 June 1944] 739 aircraft – 535 Lancasters, 165 Halifaxes, 39 Mosquitoes – from all groups attacked 7 sites, causing fresh damage at most of the targets. (The flying-bomb sites were now becoming so cratered by RAF, 8th Air

Force and 2nd Tactical Air Force bombing that results for individual raids were becoming difficult to determine.)

22 Lancasters were lost from these raids; it was a clear, moonlit night and most of the bomber casualties were caused by German night fighters, often operating with the help of searchlights.

Despite this work, the Vengeance threat still continued. And 30 AU was employed to do what they were meant to do and thus support Operations CROSSBOW and BIG BEN.

'Allied bombing prevented the completion of the Watten missile bunker in its intended form, and the small section completed was used for liquid oxygen production. It was abandoned in the summer of 1944 when the Pas de Calais was overrun by the British 21st Army Group.'

V2 Ballistic Missile 1942-52, Steven J. Zaloga

Operations in the Pas de Calais

On 31 August, a party under Lieutenant Commander Dalzel-Job entered Rouen ahead of all other Allied troops. The principal target was the Clinique Tambereaux, which had been the local German Headquarters. Nothing much of interest was found, so they pressed on with X Troop, Lieutenants Hugill and Besant, who were also ahead of the Allied advance.

A Troop, under Captain Huntingdon-Whitely and 2nd Lieutenant Rose, with Sub Lieutenant Long, was working up the coast. Le Touquet was taken on 9 September (but there was nothing of interest there for 30 AU). Le Havre was entered on the 12th, with 30 AU fighting their way into the harbour area. Captain Huntingdon-Whiteley and one RM OR were killed during the battle. Two other RMs were wounded. Despite the loss the harbour was taken and important documentation concerning minefields was taken. A thermal detecting installation was discovered, albeit in a damaged condition, on the headland.

Lieutenant Hugill entered the V weapon launching sites, including some monumental concrete emplacements, around Calais. These buildings were stripped down and sentries posted outside. Hugill then made detailed drawings of the buildings and launching sites, passing them quickly on to the relevant people.

Despite Hugill's efforts and the importance of his drawings, it was concluded that the methods of search were not as painstaking and complete as they might have been. This led to a criticism on the part of ACOS (I) to the effect that there was a tendency in the unit to keep pushing on to a new target instead of making a diligent investigation of objectives already captured. (Personally, I don't believe this.)

That said – and as the above work in the Pas de Calais clearly illustrates – 30 AU were blasting their way through to targets ahead of the front line and attempting to capture Naval documents (their original objective drawn up through ACOS (I) before D Day) and other material, as well as attack the V rocket installations and make them safe. It was an extremely difficult job; time consuming too. And that is where some sympathy must be extended to 30 AU: the element of surprise, coupled with speed of entry, was what gave them the opportunity to take the most secret information i.e. capture it before the enemy could destroy it.

'In late afternoon we came suddenly to the [V1] launching site, lying in eerie silence. The evening sunshine glinting through the trees lit a concrete blockhouse and "J"-shaped concrete runway, and all around were scattered hurriedly abandoned German equipment and belongings.'

Arctic Snow to Dust of Norway, Patrick Dalzel-Job

Chapter 19

Paris and the Port of Brest

On 23 August 1944, 30 AU heard reports on the BBC that Paris had fallen. Lieutenant Colonel Woolley and Captain Cunningham hurried to Le Mans where they were informed that T Force had left for Versailles at midnight on 22-23 August, with a view to an immediate entry into Paris.

Woolley attempted to reach Versailles but having discovered it was still in enemy hands, he finally found T Force near Rambouillet at 2200hrs.

Lieutenant Glanville and his RM orderly had also penetrated to the outskirts of Versailles in order to establish contact with the FFI. Eventually he met an officer of MI6 at Rambouillet and together they kept an appointment with an agent who had just come out of Paris. It was agreed that a further meeting should be held the next morning. Later, Glanville met Woolley by chance. The position was discussed and it was established that no signal had been originated by T Force calling 30 AU up to Rambouillet. A message was accordingly sent via VII US Corps Headquarters.

X Troop and the remainder of the force arrived on 25 August and a meeting was held at Rambouillet at 1000hrs. This was attended by Woolley, Captain Cunningham, Glanville, an MI6 officer and the Paris agent. The latter presented precise details of the dispositions of the enemy around Paris and indicated a route, mainly by secondary roads and field tracks, whereby a column of soft-skinned vehicles might reach the city without encountering any armour.

Woolley returned to T Force HQ at noon and was informed

that the column for Paris would move at 1400hrs. When that hour came T Force were still not ready to leave, mainly because it had no fighting troops and was not prepared for battle. In the circumstances Woolley decided to set off alone.

Lieutenant Commander Izzard was detached at this point to find US Third Army HQ in order to send off a signal to bring into action the Gambier Parry communication link with the Admiralty through MI6 in London.

At 1430hrs on 25 August, Woolforce left by road and entered Paris via St Benoit, Verrières Le Buisson and the Porte d'Orleans at 1630hrs.

When it is considered that General Le Clerc lost half his armour in reaching Paris from Rambouillet, much credit is due to Woolley's convoy.

Most of the roads in Paris were barricaded and progress was slow. Woolforce progressed to the main target, the supposed U-boat headquarters housed in a block of flats adjacent to Pont Mirabeau. Although meteorological equipment was found, the flats had mainly been used to billet the enemy troops who were 400 yards away in the headquarters of Grossadmiral Doenitz. After two hours of firing, the objective was captured by a patrol under Captain Pike.

The Troop made their way through Paris clearing similar objectives. As soon as the targets in the vicinity of the Bois de Boulogne had been captured, an expedition was fitted out to go to the torpedo arsenal, which was located in the former mushroom quarries near Houilles. This underground factory had been only partly demolished, a large part having remained intact, thanks to French workers having cut wires and fuzes leading to the charges. Attempts had also been made to destroy all torpedoes, including those in the local railway yard, by fire. The torpedo store in the tunnel at St Cloud and the accessories depot at Forte Cormeilles, in the forest of d'Herblay, were taken later and supplied a large quantity of very important documents and accessories.

The port and harbour of Brest and the surrounding countryside yielded some interesting types of equipment, including the infra-red searchlight harbour protection device from Le Gouler de Brest. In the U-boat pens at the Naval Headquarters, the Germans had made good use of the time available during the siege to destroy or otherwise dispose of their secret papers and material. Apart from burning papers their modus operandi had been to throw material into the U-boat pens, where charges were fired and the whole then flooded with fuel and sea water.

Lieutenant Commander Postlewaite and his party had joined up with a field team under Captain Frew RN and Captain Ingram USN, with whom an easy working partnership was established. The whole area was investigated and a seaborne Freya gunlaying radar apparatus, with undamaged valves, was recovered from a wrecked ship in Audierne Bay. Another interesting piece of equipment taken was the elaborate fire-control gear from the Scharhorst coastal defence battery nearby.

Since the Germans had had ample time in which to destroy their secret material, there was little justification for keeping the whole of B Troop, as well as a number of naval officers, on the Brest front, when there was so much to be done around Paris. A further criticism which was advanced later against the Brest party was that they allowed themselves to be daunted by the appalling mess in the U-boat pens, from which a substantial amount of valuable equipment was eventually recovered by salvage parties. On the other hand it is only fair to point out that 30 AU's team was not equipped at this time for heavy salvage work.

This work ended the first phase of 30 AUs participation in Operation OVERLORD. By the end of September 1944, the whole unit had been recalled to reform and refit for duties in Germany, due to begin in November.

It was during the refit time that the Black List was updated and distributed. This was probably written from the summary list of 30 AU achievements during the first period of OVERLORD. The information concerning V rockets and their installations had been very important and led to a better understanding of these dangerous weapons by British scientists, which allowed Alanbrooke – and others – to form strong arguments to knock out such sites using the RAF. Add to that the information concerning torpedoes, mines, high-speed morse and pulse transmission (radar and WT), optics, and most importantly the locations of the German Admiralty, 30 AU were now seen to have really proved their worth and were now an important part of the OVERLORD operations.

Chapter 20

The V Rocket Vendetta

'The concentration of heavy and light *flak* from Den Helder to the Scheldt was our daily experience, and later we learned that no less than 200 batteries of well-manned guns would lie in our path.'

Tales of My Time, Raymond Baxter

The problem with writing a unit history is only putting several pieces of a puzzle on the table, i.e. the bits of a complex operation applicable just to them. So this chapter continues to move away from 30 AU to concentrate on what others were doing (namely RAF Spitfire squadrons) concerning V rockets. This chapter clearly shows the importance of 30 AU's work in the bigger scheme of things.

Raymond Baxter stated in *Operation Big Ben* (Spellmount, 2004) that the intelligence they (602 Squadron) got from their sources wasn't exactly a flood! Ground intelligence was extremely important too. There was the smattering of spies who worked their trade across Europe, but more important was the quality technical information that came from commando units, specifically Woolforce in 30 AU. They had properly analysed the first V1 site with their scientists and fed that information back; then, according to the veterans, they were given the task of seeking out other V1 and V2 rocket sites and getting that information home too. We know there were many more than one V1 site because Patton stated that when he joined the

OVERLORD campaign: 'The whole northern tip of Cherbourg Peninsula was covered with launching sites for V1 bombs. These were very interesting.'

30 AU (Woolforce) knew that the work they were doing was essential to the well-being of civilians in London and the Home Counties. Around them, Lancaster bombers (or a select few) and Spitfires dive-bombed, Mosquitoes flew suicide missions, spies risked life and limb single-handedly and the commando units aggressively attacked behind enemy lines or, at least, in the front line of attack, after D-Day.

30 AU started to get a little too big for their boots, as the following anecdote clearly illustrates: Commander Fleming gave Dunstan Curtis a detailed list of desirable pieces of equipment for 30 AU to acquire during their raids. Again, this was to separate their work from other commando units. If they could recover certain items and get them sent back to the Admiralty, it would help with the gathering of important intelligence and provide a solution to counter enemy activity.

30 AU became a tenacious bunch, so much so that Fleming gave them the nickname '30 Indecent Assault Unit'.

On 15 August 1943, Fleming received a message from Curtis. He explained that important radar equipment had been captured by the unit at Douvres-la-Deliverande and was ready for transport back to Britain.

Fleming organized a high-speed launch to hop across the Channel the following night to pick up the equipment and bring it home. Unfortunately the launch returned from Cherbourg without its bounty. 30 AU had forgotten all about it.

Fleming was outraged by this slapdash attitude. Suddenly it appeared that certain officers were getting a little too big for their boots. Fleming channelled his disgust through the following message:

Great trouble was taken to lay this craft on as you desired and it is indeed disappointing that the unit should have failed ... in its side of the arrangements ... to put it mildly, DDOD (I) is fed up to the back teeth ... I urge you not to continue questioning the decisions of DNI ... under whose orders you operate. The position in Brittany and also in regard to Paris is perfectly clear here and we are fully informed on the progress of the campaign. Why you should imagine that this is not so, which is the only possible excuse for your attitude, I cannot understand.[1] The duties of the unit and its immediate role are also planned on the basis of more information than you can ever possess in the field.

One thing is certain and that is that unless the unit obeys its orders without question during the future stages of the campaign it will be impossible for me or Captain Lewes to prevent higher authority intervening drastically.

30 AU had been left to their own devices a little too long. They had formed opinions, made assumptions and plotted their own plans to an extent where they continued to think for themselves when orders arrived. Little was more important than their work at the coalface – Whitehall had got things wrong and the Admiralty was just hot air and red tape. Well, that's what they thought until Commander Fleming's message arrived and put them firmly in their place. The threats were there and the belittling comment explaining that NID held more intelligence than they could ever have in the field was a schoolteacher talking down to pupil. But it was needed and, like any good commando unit, they responded positively to the reprimand.

'I told him about the V2 rockets which had started to land in England, and from whence they came. He said he had always intended to give priority to the Ruhr thrust and the northern route of advance, and that this was being done. I said that it was not being done.'

The Memoirs of Field Marshal Montgomery

Chapter 21

Conquering Europe

'Meanwhile Germany crumbles. The Italian front has surrendered, Monty takes 100,000 prisoners, Hamburg gives in and negotiations with Monty look like the rest of Northern Germany and Denmark giving in!'

Diary entry 3 May 1945, *War Diaries 1939-1945, Field Marshal Lord Alanbrooke*, edited by Alex Danchev and Daniel Todman

From the beginning of July the main body of 30 AU were encamped in the Headquarters near Carteret. Effectively they were disposing of the bounty captured so far, crating and sending it on its onward journey to be analysed, while at the same time making repairs to their vehicles.

DNI and Commander Fleming made a quick visit. They put a little more organization to the cataloguing of some of the documentation and equipment being shipped. They informed the unit that Lieutenant Glanville and Miss Margaret Priestly (Admiralty civilian officer) were planning future operations, while scientists were being trained for the advance into Germany.

Interestingly, one of Glanville's more adventurous plans was to attach troops of AU personnel to the SAS and parachute them in behind enemy lines at strategic points to capture material from the Germans as they moved, so there would be no danger of them destroying valuable documentation before the ground party moved in. X Troop was brought back to Britain to undergo parachute training to support this idea but it was never fully exploited.

With regard to the planning of the capture of Paris, a formation known as T Force had been set up by SHAEF to handle all intelligence targets in the area. Glanville was accordingly appointed 30 AU Liaison Officer to T Force with the object of ensuring that high-grade naval objectives in the area should be handled by 30 AU. This did not prove an easy task, for an organization called the Combined Intelligence Objectives Sub-Committee (CIOS) had been set up under SHAEF to organize and control the capture and exploitation of all targets of intelligence value in enemy controlled territory. The Admiralty was represented on this sub-committee by Mr Evershed of DSR, who was in close touch with NID 30 and who was generally in favour of leaving 30 AU to handle all naval targets other than those of an advanced scientific or technical nature. These, he considered, should also be captured by 30 AU but kept under guard until such time as they could be examined by scientists. COIS and T Force inclined to the view that if 30 AU was to participate in these operations at all it should do so only as a part of T Force, and that it should conform to the internal rules and regulations of the formation.

COIS had produced their own black list of target areas and 30 AU's revised list was incorporated into that as the Naval Section.

During this period, while the capture of Paris was being planned, an interminable series of meetings was held at SHAEF at which procedures were discussed. Briefly the scheme envisaged was that combat troops should enter the area and seize all known intelligence objectives, after which the combat engineers would advance and remove or make safe all booby traps, mines and time bombs. Then the investigators would be called forwards and escorted to their targets. All documents and material on the premises were to be listed on special forms and eventually crated and shipped to appropriate destinations by troops specially detailed for the purpose.

It was pointed out to the T Force planning committee that the proposed scheme contained a number of flaws, including the possibility that headquarters and other objectives might have moved since the date of the most recent intelligence. Also, the fact that targets often had to be fought for and consequently that specially trained troops, such as 30 AU, were required to ensure that valuable documents and material were not lost by fire, or during the process of their capture.

Finally, after much discussion and argument, and largely as the result of pressure brought to bear by DNI through Commander Fleming, it was agreed that 30 AU should be allowed to handle an agreed list of naval targets in the Paris area, provided: Firstly, that clearance was retained from T Force before any material was shipped to the UK; and Secondly, that they should submit a daily report on the activities to T Force, with a copy for SHAEF.

A list of the more important naval targets was accordingly compiled and submitted for comment to the NID geographical section concerned, and also to MI6, who undertook to lay on special enquiries in order to obtain the latest information. Plans of the buildings concerned were obtained from ISTD and carefully annotated maps made of the surroundings. Particular attention was paid to the possibility of organizing a parachute drop near the Bois de Boulogne, around which the most important naval targets were situated.

Meanwhile the military situation was developing quickly and, in view of the successful landing and rapid advance of the US Second Army, it was decided to cancel the arrangements made for a series of parachute descents on the Brest Peninsula and to concentrate on the exploitation of the Atlantic U-boat ports by A and B Troops, starting from Carterest, and an airborne attack by X Troop on the German U-boat headquarters in Paris.

While all this was in progress, a number of Admiralty civilian scientists and technical officers who had volunteered for special duties in Germany underwent a brief course of training at Littlehampton and London.

It must be clearly understood that during the operations leading up to the capture of Cherbourg, 30 AU was the only British unit working in the US sector. This caused frustrations for them as they were treated with some suspicion by the Americans. They mentioned their problems to Commander Fleming when he briefly arrived at Carteret. He promised to raise the issue of a general signal being issued to the US Army commanders from SHAEF, explaining the functions of 30 AU and instructing them to give the unit as much freedom as possible.

Despite this hiccup, permission was granted for Dalzel-Job, Lessing, Captain Douglas and Captain Wheeler to take part in the capture of Granville.

On 31 July, the team left Carteret and entered Granville with the leading formations. A thorough search was made of the port and naval installations, but nothing of any value was found. The harbour had not been used during the two weeks prior to the fall of Cherbourg, and the harbour works had been thoroughly demolished.

It was on 1 August that DNI's influence was felt – through Fleming – in SHAEF, as a signal was received. It was signed by none other than General Eisenhower and was addressed to Commander First US Army instructing the latter to arrange for the employment of 30 AU in the capture of targets of naval intelligence interest in Brittany, the details of the unit's operations to be arranged on the spot with the local commanders involved.

It seemed that Fleming and DNI arranged things pretty well for 30 AU by getting General Eisenhower's authority and, frankly, things became more comfortable for the unit from thereafter. Targets from Avranches to Vannes were dealt with in a more systematic way. Not long afterwards 30 AU completed a full, single-handed raid on the complex of buildings that was the U-boat headquarters around the Chateau de Pignerolles, near Angers.

On 11 August, Commander Curtis had a conference with Lieutenant Colonel Woolley to discuss plans for handling the U-boats near Angers. At the same time the first official contact was made with the US Naval Task Force 125.8, which consisted mainly of investigating officers, who were doing work of a generally similar nature to that of 30 AU. Contacts between the unit and this task force had been frequent since the beginning of the attack on Cherbourg and relationships had been set up between the officers (probably with General Eisenhower's signal in mind). Despite being ordered to get along, 30 AU teamed well with the Americans.

That said, the problems with communications with 30 AU and outside forces was really to do with their British chain of command. NID didn't really know what they were doing all the time or their official chain of command, which was why Colonel H. Quill RM was appointed their Formation Commander. This did cause some jealousy between the echelons of the unit, but that was to be expected.

On 15 August, the officers commanding the two wings of the unit held a conference at the rear headquarters and discussed plans for the participation of 30 AU in the capture of Paris. It was decided that, if possible, the main target should be approached by a parachute descent, and for this purpose Lieutenant Colonel Woolley, who had recently qualified as a parachutist, should return to the UK together with Captain Pike and X Troop, in order to report to the airfield selected for the operational take-off. It was further agreed that Lieutenant Glanville should be in charge of the naval section of the force, which was to include Lieutenant Besant, who had completed a mission at Saint Malo, Sub Lieutenant Long and Lieutenant Commander Izzard (the latter as an interrogator).

The whole force assembled at Littlehampton while the finishing touches were put to the planning in the Admiralty. It was planned that the main attack was to centre around the complex of buildings constituting the U-boat headquarters in the Bois de Boulogne. Glanville was to jump twenty-four hours ahead of the rest of the force, in order to make contacts and signal back through Special Forces Headquarters in London, with a time for the rest of the team to jump. They would then make their way to Paris.

The SAS and MI6 spoke about a time for Glanville to drop but despite their persistence over three separate nights the weather was too bad and it was decided to do the whole operation by land.

Chapter 22

The Enemy Begins to Crumble

'We now come to momentous days.'

The Memoirs of Field Marshal Montgomery

The whole party, which was known as Woolforce II, embarked at Portsmouth on 17 August and arrived next morning at Arromaches.

30 AU pushed forward slowly but as soon as they arrived at targets in the immediate vicinity of the Bois de Boulogne and had dealt with them, an expedition was fitted out to go to the torpedo arsenal (west), which was located in the former mushroom quarries near Houilles. This underground factory had been only partly demolished, a large part having remained intact through French workers having cut wires and fuzes leading to the charges. Attempts had also been made to destroy all torpedoes, including those in the local railway yard, by fire.

Items of much interest were found around this area, both documents and equipment classified at Top Secret level. As the unit progressed to Paris so much more was uncovered and the real operational requirement of the unit finally fulfilled. Despite the resistance of others, NID/DNI had kept things ticking over and now the rewards were there in abundance. As the Germans slowly got used to the fact that they had finally been beaten, more and more intelligence came to 30 AU's attention.

Some might argue that it might have all been a little too late, but that is not the case at all. When the war was over, an operation was set up so Germany couldn't achieve the level of intelligence/engineering skill it had obtained since the end of the First World War to the outbreak of the Second World War. 30 AU were largely responsible for spiriting away all the stores of intelligence that had been gathered in disparate areas of Europe to achieve this operation's aims. Of course, most of the ground work was done by the unit in the run-up to the close of the war, especially in the Pas de Calais from 31 August to the end of September where the whole of the unit had been recalled to reform and refit for special duties in Germany. The first phase of OVERLORD was now completely finished. The verdict of Naval Intelligence concerning 30 AU's work was 'fruitful', little else – despite the heartache.

The date originally given by 21st Army Group for the beginning of the collapse of Germany was 1 November 1944 and, as a consequence, preparations were made in considerable haste. In view of the peculiar conditions anticipated in Germany, which was expected to involve guerrilla fighting and widespread sabotage, coupled with the commitment of 30 AU to provide accommodation and bodyguards for a substantial number of Admiralty scientists, the headquarters staff of the RM wing was considerably strengthened. At the same time, twenty-seven RM drivers were drafted to the unit to look after the additional motor transport which had been obtained.

It soon become apparent that 1 November was premature as a date for the 'beginning of the collapse of Germany' and this was altered initially to the first week in December, and subsequently to various dates in early 1945.

In these circumstances 30 AU was not represented in the capture of Walcheren Island or in the airborne attacks on Arnhem, Nijmegen and Eindhoven. The relative decision was made by ACOS (I) on the grounds that men and vehicles were tired and needed rest and special preparations before taking a leading part in the liquidation of the German Naval machine. This view was sound up to a point, but took no account of the need for obtaining up-to-date operational intelligence in regard to enemy minefields and coastal defences, and the movements of German Naval Headquarters and Admiralty divisions.

In November 1944, Colonel Quill was appointed to take command of 30 AU as part of their final reorganization. He spent the first few weeks in his new post enquiring into the organization and administration of the unit, with particular reference to simplifying the relations of the unit with CCO, Command Group, the RMO and other authorities to whom it owed allegiance, and in establishing a clear and unequivocal chain of command.

This problem had become more difficult at this time than ever before, since ACOS (I) to ANCXF had gradually assumed the functions of a formation commander. He was issuing directives to the officers in charge of the wings in connection with the internal administration and discipline of the unit. Meanwhile dual allegiance of the RN wing to CCO and DNI, and of the RM wing to GOC Commando Group, was beginning to cause a substantial measure of confusion in the internal economics of the unit.

Quill changed round the personnel and went back to Europe in December 1944 with naval targets firmly in his sights. These operations proved profitable, particularly in regard to the new submarine programme. On the other hand, certain of the parties concerned had not behaved well in the field and had brought 30 AU into serious disrepute with higher authorities. As usual the RM fraternity had misbehaved and, slightly less worrying, the unit was accused of arriving in a town late at night, without having given previous warning, demanding quarters, rations and canteen stores. That said, 30 AU were noted as getting on very well with the French!

'While Charles Wheeler was talking to a Frenchman in the garden of the chateau, an American soldier in a passing truck picked up his rifle and shot the Frenchman, who died in Charles' arms.'

Reminiscence of Patrick Dalzel-Job, *Attain by Surprise* (edited by David Nutting)

Chapter 23

From the End to PAPERCLIP

'Thus finished our Combined Chiefs of Staff Meeting, in
Berlin!! where we had never hoped to meet in our wildest
dreams in the early stages of this war. And now that we are
here I feel too weary and cooked to even get a kick out of it. It
all feels flat and empty. I am feeling very tired and worn out.'

Diary entry, 24 July 1945, *War Diaries 1939-1945, Field Marshal
Lord Alanbrooke*, edited by Alex Danchev and Daniel Todman

It is fairly common knowledge that 30 AU captured the whole of
the German Navy Archive and, as they pushed ever forwards,
more important naval targets concerning U-boat manufacturing
sites and associated intelligence.

To conclude this history I don't want to focus on this aspect as
that is laid down quite nicely in books such as *Attain by Surprise*,
edited by David Nutting (David Colver Publisher, 1997, 2003)
and, of course in Patrick Dalzel-Job's autobiography. I want to
focus on that exclusive position enjoyed by 30 AU within the
American forces and how they completed their war before
disbandment in early 1946.

It is known by members of 30 AU and myself that there are
still certain things that cannot be said about the unit, particularly
appertaining to V rocket intelligence. If it is true that 30 AU
captured the V rocket scientists and the commanding American
forces took over, then we can blame General Eisenhower for
starting NASA and the resulting Cold War (*sic*).

Of course, it is not as clear cut as that: the Russians were involved – that's why they had their cut too – and that's what really started the Cold War.

What I am highlighting here is the need for more information to complete this history – the history veterans want to document but the powers-that-be still shy away from, including the late Ian Fleming himself.

The importance of 30 AU was never fully appreciated by the politicians and Chiefs-of-Staff – if it was, the war would have been concluded in a more satisfactory way. And read into that what you want.

For Dalzel-Job the war concluded well. As soon as it was over he quickly returned home and married his sweetheart.

'Get as far as they could the first night, away from Pas de Calais ... Was he getting serious about this girl?'

Moonraker, Ian Fleming

Afterword

'Shortly after the fighting in Europe stopped ... Patrick [Dalzel-Job], determined to end the war where, for him, it had begun, had persuaded the Navy to put his jeep and its crew on a destroyer bound for Norway. There he had left a girl, waving from the quayside ... within a few days there was a wedding, followed by a blissfully happy naval and civilian life.'

From Charles Wheeler's Foreword to *Arctic Snow to Dust of Normandy* by Patrick Dalzel-Job

I'm told that at a certain time of year – every year – somebody walks into The Marine Public House, Littlehampton, and places a flag to 30 AU at the foot of their memorial. This person leaves before the landlord can question him, but then again, he doesn't really feel the urge to do so. It's just a moment of respect, a beautiful moment of tranquillity, which acknowledges the work the unit did – to this day, unseen and unappreciated.

The story you have just read is one about a real-life, front-line, Top Secret team of commandos, a group of men who fought hard to win the peace. Some of them were maimed and killed, others survived. What I find unforgivable is the lack of acknowledgement given to 30 AU over the years, to their tenacity and dedication. Even with names such as Charles Wheeler and Patrick Dalzel-Job the unit hasn't reached the level of fame and respect it deserves. That said, I must admit that I came across the unit through the wartime work of Ian Fleming, but they suddenly took on a life and importance all of their own to me – simply put, they did something Fleming only dreamed of doing.

When I read of the many deaths of individuals in the field – people whose life story I had been reading every day – I felt saddened to lose them. To me their personalities shone through – their highs, their lows, the blood, sweat and tears of their daily toll. I find the unit history of 30 AU one of courage and determination, amidst frustration and exhaustion. I sincerely hope that one day they get the statue they so richly deserve and a place in the hearts of all future generations, rather than just be another largely overlooked group of individuals forgotten and unappreciated.

Annexe A

From V Rockets to Moonraker

'The V2's trajectory was more like a shell fired from a gun. At the top of its 200-mile flight it had climbed to about 70 miles. It was fuelled with a very combustible mixture of alcohol and liquid oxygen which was watered down so as not to burn out the mild steel which 'was all they were allocated for the engine.'

Moonraker, Ian Fleming

I first wrote about 30 AU and V rockets in my book *Ian Fleming's Secret War*. It was a response to what the veterans of 30 AU told me about their V rocket experiences in relation to what the archives didn't tell me! I don't want to go into conspiracy theories here and fall into the trap of speculating that a host of information is buried deep within the archives, or was destroyed after the war. What I decided to do in my last book was look at Ian Fleming's interests in V rockets through the novel *Moonraker*. This presented me with many coincidences with regard to 30 AU, V rockets and Ian Fleming; things that shouldn't be overlooked.

I present a fresh look at the material I previously gathered in this Annexe in order to tap into a very dark area of 30 AU's history through the eyes of literature, biography and interview. It lays foundations for future research that the general historian would perhaps overlook. Also, and most importantly, it addresses what the veterans of 30 AU considered to be a very

important and time-consuming part of their war: the 30 AU V
rocket campaigns.

'All young men and women, of any intelligence at all, on some
occasion or other decide that they would like to write. In the
destructive environment of war the creative urge to write is
wholly reasonable, especially writing of the type Cheshire
enjoyed, a playing of words and a delight in fantasy.'

Cheshire VC, Russell Braddon

So what did the 30 AU veterans say about their V rocket
campaigns? First, I asked them about their involvement in
Operations CROSSBOW, BIG BEN and PAPERCLIP, the three
essential operations connected with Britain's fight against the V
rockets. I asked them about the occasional bit of intelligence that
filtered through concerning V rockets and how they dealt with it.

I was told that there was so much intelligence and,
consequently, work, connected with the V1s and V2s, 30 AU had
their own specialist (Ralph Izzard) who was so important his
Number 2 was told to kill him if he fell into enemy hands! I was
also told that 30 AU had scientists attached to their sections who
were there solely to assess the evidence of V rockets. This shows
an in-depth analysis of V rockets going on within the unit, but a
serious lack of documentation being generated. Such relevant
information directly sourced from the veterans concerning 30
AU's V rocket campaigns must count.

That said, in his book *Arctic Snow to Dust of Normandy*, Patrick
Dalzel-Job did present one tantalizing V1 story: he explained
that it was in early June 1944 that he took a squad of Royal
Marines through a gap in enemy lines to seek out a V1 rocket site
that had been identified by the RAF. His squad took a team of
'experts' to the site later that day (the scientists referred to by the
veterans I spoke with?), the very day the first V1 fell on London.

The veterans also explained to me – and in slight contradiction
maybe to Dalzel-Job – that Fleming told 30 AU where the V
rocket sites were located. They suggested that he might have got

his information through the French Resistance. We know that Dalzel-Job worked with the French Resistance, with some assistance from Staff-Sergeant Bramah, and said in his book that the French Resistance were dramatically underused during the war, but he used them, and Fleming may have used them too.

None of the above is supposition. It is all first-hand knowledge or first-hand opinion from the people who were there. So we know categorically that Commander Fleming/30 AU had something more than a passing interest in the V rocket campaigns.

Why is this information important? Simply because if the most extreme rumours are correct, it was 30 AU who captured Wernher von Braun and Domberger in Bavaria at the end of the war. This I cannot substantiate, because if it is true it rewrites the history books and throws up many questions appertaining to the splitting up of Nazi scientists after the war (Operation PAPERCLIP). It is known that some scientists – including von Braun – went to America and worked on the rocket campaigns that led to NASA. It is known that some scientists went to Russia and started work on their rocket campaigns (and effectively started the space race, the Cold War and the battle of the 'superpowers'), and it is believed that 100 scientists worked for Britain under Operation SURGEON (a post-war program to exploit German aeronautics and deny German technical skills to Russia). So all this information is very important to our understanding of how V rockets, their scientists and the governments of America, Russia and Britain forged the second half of the twentieth century, through flight, nuclear power, the space race and, consequently, the Cold War.

'"Fifty of these are German," continued M. "More or less all the guided missile experts the Russians didn't get. Drax paid for them to come over here and work on the *Moonraker*. Nobody was very happy with the arrangements but there was no alternative."'

Moonraker, Ian Fleming

But how does this information, the facts as we know them, work in relation to Ian Fleming and *Moonraker* (and ostensibly 30 AU)?

In the novel there are fifty Nazi scientists who work for Sir Hugo Drax in creating the Moonraker rocket. The rocket is described as a silver cigar-shaped missile, similar to the V2. The base for the rocket in the novel is the White Cliffs of Dover.

So going back to the true story, you have 100 scientists who opted to work for Britain having worked on the V rockets. Also, there are conspiracy theorists who believe that some scientists worked in chalk tunnels at Alum Bay, Isle of Wight, which is a direct comparison to the White Cliffs of Dover in *Moonraker*. However, I don't believe this because a chalk tunnel from the fort above Alum Bay was cut many years before the Second World War and that is meant to be one of the clinching pieces of evidence in support of that theory. Also, it is known that Ian Fleming had to ask people[1] about the scientific issues associated with the Moonraker in his novel – he didn't possess the information himself. This shows that if 30 AU had a real hands-on operation connected in some way to Operation PAPERCLIP or Operation SURGEON (no later than 1946), then Fleming probably didn't. Indeed, he hung up his boots towards the end of 1945 before the main thrust of PAPERCLIP, and certainly before Operation SURGEON kicked in.

What is interesting is the ground work laid down by Fleming from Operation CROSSBOW through to Operation BIG BEN. 30 AU received intelligence from Fleming, we are told (he got some of this from the French Resistance, we believe). We also know that the RAF supplied information and we know that Fleming studied aerial photographs. Clearly he must have worked through the SOE (Sir Colin Gubbins) to the Crossbow Committee, thus sharing his ground-work exercises through 30 AU to help the dive-bombing Spitfire missions that made up Operation BIG BEN.

Is there any evidence that 30 AU was physically involved in Operation PAPERCLIP-type work?

Yes, going back to Ralph Izzard, we know that he received the address of a professor of liquid oxygen in a house near Tours towards the end of the war, so that is direct intelligence and recovery of a suspect. And it is for all this ground work leading up to and including the first steps of Operation PAPERCLIP that veterans of 30 AU thank Ian Fleming for. They say that the importance of stopping the V1s and V2s was tantamount to the success of the unit as a whole. The V rockets were the first terrorist attacks on London – a direct attack on civilian lives – and 30 AU labour this point to this day. They took pride in the work they did at the coalface under all things V rocket related (they probably were not aware of the operational code words that have been associated with this work but certainly remember carrying out the tasks associated with them). They marvelled as to where Fleming got his intelligence from, because they maintain that he was right time after time and then, in the next breath, they express their sadness that, despite all the work he did under this incredibly important operational requirement, he was not credited for his major roll countering the threat and closing the sites down (and arresting the scientists). But let us look more closely at *Moonraker*. After James Bond thwarts Sir Hugo Drax's plan to blow up London with his Vengeance-style rocket, Bond receives a thank you – through M – from the Prime Minister; but he receives no award (unlike the lady who worked with him). M reminds Bond that in their covert line of work, one doesn't receive those sorts of awards (a George Cross in the novel). Does this scene emanate in real life for Fleming? It is difficult to tell. There is a distinct lack of evidence, which is why this piece resides as an Annexe to my book and not an historical chapter. I am using a blend of fact and fiction to make a plausible argument that Fleming and 30 AU played a significant part in Operations PAPERCLIP and SURGEON or, at least, laid significant foundations in Operations CROSSBOW and BIG BEN.

Veterans from 30 AU mention that most officers were decorated after the war who had operational duties in 30 AU, and they also stated that certain parts of the unit didn't know what other parts were doing – now, with many veterans dead, their work is largely unappreciated. I certainly believe 30 AU/Ian Fleming had much to do with V rockets, I believe the evidence is there and I believe that they should get some credit for carrying out that most secret work.

Is that all?

No, not quite. To add more relevance to the comparison between *Moonraker* and *Ian Fleming's Secret War*, there are historical, albeit slightly fictionalized for Drax's sake, accounts of Otto Skorzeny's work . We know that Fleming was fascinated by Skorzeny and took the mindset of his intelligence-gathering commandos for the creation of 30 AU. So there you have a comparison directly relevant to Fleming's Red Indians. Skorzeny is mentioned by name in the book but I don't believe he was the model for Sir Hugo Drax, because Fleming makes Drax one of Skorzeny's men and his physical appearance is nothing like the historical character.

So through *Moonraker*, Fleming gives us the source of 30 AU, Nazi scientists, V rockets, all from a British angle, not American. There is a brief mention of Russian technology in the form of a submarine that takes Drax away towards the end of the book; but then there is the dissatisfaction of Bond at the end that could emanate from Fleming's own feelings regarding the lack of recognition of his work for the war effort.

So in conclusion, there are strands of evidence that allow us to make tantalizing comparisons but little else. I for one do believe that 30 AU – not necessarily Ian Fleming – had much to do with thwarting the V rocket threat and bringing the guilty to justice.

'Professor Train had walked up to a row of huge wall maps and had pulled down the cord of one of them. Bond was faced with a ten-foot horizontal scale diagram of something that looked like a V2 with big fins.'

Moonraker, Ian Fleming

Annexe B

The Men of 30 Assault Unit

(In alphabetical order, surname, initials and rank if known, notes of wounded and killed in action)

Armitage, Lieutenant Commander
Ashton, Private (killed in action)
Austen, Mr (scientist)
Bailey, Lieutenant, RM
Ballentyne, Lieutenant (on loan for European operations from US Forces)
Bancroft, Corporal (died of wounds received in action)
Belcher, T., Captain
Besant, J., Lieutenant
Blake, Lance Corporal
Cass, Major
Coates, J.G., Captain
Cunningham, Captain
Curtis, Lieutenant (later Lieutenant Commander and Commander)
Dalzel-Job, P., Lieutenant Commander
Davies, D.N., Lieutenant, RNVR
Douglas, Captain
Edwards, Private, Army
Ellington, Corporal
Evans, A.L., Major, RM
Glanville, T.J., Lieutenant, Army (after transfer from RN)

Gray, H.R., Surgeon Lieutenant
Hargreaves-Heap, Captain
Heath, Private, Army
Hill, T., Captain
Hugill, Lieutenant
Huntingdon-Whiteley, Captain, RM (killed in action)
Ionides, Lieutenant (killed in action)
Kruthoffer, J., Sergeant, RM
Lamb, Captain (wounded in action)
Lambie, Lieutenant (on loan for European operations from US Forces)
Levant, Staff Officer (Intelligence)
Levy, Private (King's Corporal of the Field)
Lincoln, F.A., Lieutenant Commander, RNVR
Long, Sub Lieutenant (later Lieutenant) (wounded in action)
MacGreggor, Captain
Macleman, Private (wounded in action)
McDavid, Private (killed in action)
McFee, Lieutenant (later Lieutenant Commander)
McGrath, P., RM
Martin-Smith, Captain, Army
Mayers, Lance Corporal
Ogle, J., Lieutenant, RNVR
Orton, Lieutenant
Philips, C.W.H.J., Lieutenant, RNVR
Postlewaite, Lieutenant Commander
Powell, J.
Riley, Q.T.P., Lieutenant Commander
Rinway, Private
Ryder, Red, Commander, RN
Shermuly, Corporal
Tamplin, Lieutenant, RNVR
Taylor, Lieutenant, Army
Taylor, S.H., Mr (scientist)
Tewson, Lieutenant
Thomas, B.
Tucker, S., Lieutenant, Army

Van Cleef, Lieutenant
Ward, H.R., Lieutenant Commander (later Commander) RNVR
Ward, J.A., Captain, Army
Wheeler, Charles, Lieutenant Commander
Whitby, Sergeant
Wilkinson, Staff Sergeant (lost leg in action)
Woolley, Lieutenant Colonel
Wright, Corporal (killed in action)
Wright, B., RM

Annexe C

30 Assault Unit Officer Profiles

What follows are some general personality profiles of some the officers in 30 Assault Unit, presented in alphabetical order. The list is not exhaustive, but simply serves to add personality to some of the names listed in this book and shows clearly their diverse backgrounds and expertise.

Lieutenant Commander Armitage was an amateur yachtsman before the war and had come from the sea to serve in Lis. He was awarded the GC for outstanding gallantry in dismantling enemy mines and bombs.

Lieutenant Besant graduated in modern languages at Glasgow University. After being commissioned in the RNVR he served for a time in landing craft. He was bilingual in French and English and fluent in Spanish and Portuguese. He also possessed a fair knowledge of Japanese and for this he was originally selected for service in the Pacific, although he remained in Europe.

Lieutenant Curtis graduated at Oxford and completed his studies on the Continent. He became a solicitor in 1935, joined the RNVSR in 1936 and was called up to the RNVR in February 1940. He served at first in Coastal Forces and took part in the raids on St Nazaire and Dieppe. For his part in the former he received the immediate award of the DSC. Subsequently he was engaged in special operations in home waters with DDOD(I) and joined 30 Commando on its formation. Lieutenant Curtis was fluent in French and German.

Lieutenant Commander Dalzel-Job received part of his education in Switzerland, after which he had been at sea, as a private yachtsman, in an ocean-going brigantine, mainly in Norwegian waters. He took part in the Norwegian campaign of 1940 and the final evacuation of Narvik. For these services he was awarded the Norwegian Order of Saint Olaf. He subsequently took part in various operations in northern waters with coastal forces. Fluent in Norwegian and with a working knowledge of French and German, he was appointed to 30 AU with the primary object of handling targets in Norway. Lieutenant Commander Dalzel-Job was qualified as a parachutist, deep-sea diver and had the distinction of being able to ski backwards.

Sub Lieutenant McFee was an Incorporated Accountant and at the outbreak of war held a position in the Accounts Department of the City Treasurer of Dundee. He joined the RNVR under the 'Y' scheme, and on receiving his commission volunteered for hazardous service. As a consequence he was posted to 30 Commando, where he became one of their most tenacious officers.

Commander Ian Lancaster Fleming was born on 28 May 1908 at 27 Green Street off Park Lane.[1] He was educated at Eton. After a short period at the Royal Military Academy at Sandhurst, he went abroad to continue his education. He joined Reuters News Agency in 1931 after failing to join the Foreign Office.

During the Second World War, he was personal assistant to the Director of Naval Intelligence (DNI) and learned much about covert operations and the intricacies of cipher messaging. He was also the creator and inspiration of 30 Assault Unit (30 AU), a crack team of commandos who penetrated enemy territory to gather vital intelligence and feed it back to NID. After the war he became Foreign Manager of Kemsley Newspapers and his earliest hardback book contribution was a chapter in the *Kemsley Manual of Journalism* (Cassell, 1950) concerning the work of a foreign correspondent. He published some other miscellaneous articles, but it wasn't until the age of forty-two, on the eve of his marriage, that he wrote the first James Bond novel *Casino Royale* (Jonathan Cape, 1953).

Rear Admiral John Godfrey was born in Handsworth, Birmingham, in July 1888. John Henry Godfrey was educated at King Edward Grammar School, Birmingham, and later at Bradfield College. He became a naval cadet in 1903, serving on HMS *Britannia*. He rose steadily through the ranks and during the First World War (1916) he was promoted to lieutenant commander and served in the Mediterranean and Black Sea (1917-19). He was mentioned in despatches around this time and awarded the Légion d'Honneur and the Order of the Nile. He was promoted to commander in 1920 and took several desk jobs before being appointed second-in-command of a ship in New Zealand (1925-8). He was promoted to captain on his return and became Deputy Director Staff College (1929-31). After that he commanded HMS *Suffolk* in the China Station (1931-3). He returned as Deputy Director Plans Division (1933-6) before taking command of HMS *Repulse* in the Mediterranean (1936-8). He then became DNI and rear admiral from February 1939 and resided in Room 38, behind a green baize door, accessed from Room 39.[2] He became the man who would endorse Ian Fleming's idea of an intelligence assault unit and demand that it remain part of the Naval Intelligence Division.

Lieutenant Hugill obtained a double first in natural science at Oxford. He had been working, also at Oxford, on research into nuclear physics and at the beginning of the war had been doing special work for DNOR. In 1942 he was appointed to be ANA at HM Embassy, Lisbon, where he served until December 1943. He was fluent in French and Portuguese.

Lieutenant Ionides had been a midshipman, RN during the First World War, but had resigned his commission in 1920. He had since been in business as an East India Merchant and had joined the RNVR early in the war. He had served for some years in DTM (I) as an expert on enemy mining. He could speak French and German.

Lieutenant Commander Postlewaite was an amateur yachtsman with a mechanical mind who had served at the beginning of the war in the River Thames Fire Service. Previously he had been employed by a firm of advertising agents. He joined the RNVR in 1941 and had since been serving on the staff of DTM (I) as a torpedo expert. He could speak French.

Lieutenant Tamplin had been on the staff of the Traffic Manager of LPTB before the war. He joined the RNVR in 1939 and after commissioning served in HMS *Galatea* until she was sunk. After that he served under SOI Levant in the Middle East and Mediterranean, returning to the UK early in 1944.

Lieutenant Tewson had been a professional crewman in an ocean-going yacht in which he had travelled extensively, including a long cruise in the Pacific. He had little or no military training.

Lieutenant Commander Riley was a graduate of Cambridge University. Between 1930 and 1937 he was engaged continuously on Polar exploration, taking part in two expeditions to Greenland and one to the Antarctic. He joined the RNVR in 1939 but was transferred temporarily to a special battalion of the Scots Guards, which had been mobilized to operate in Finland. This campaign did not materialize, however, and Lieutenant Commander Riley returned to the RNVR serving on the staff of Brigadier Gubbins in Norway where he was mentioned in despatches. On his return he was appointed to Combined Operations as a Flotilla Officer and eventually served in Iceland as instructor in winter warfare. On his recovery from injuries received in this service, he was selected by Commander Ryder for 30 Commando.

Lieutenant Commander Ward was educated at Eton and

qualified as a pilot in the RNAS in the First World War. He was taken prisoner by the Germans, subsequently making his escape. Between the wars he was largely engaged in social work as a visitor to prisoners and Borstal institutions. He joined the RNVR in 1939 and for the first four years of the war was engaged in lecturing Naval personnel on escape practices.

Notes

Chapter 1

1. Enclosure 1 to ADM 223/500 in National Archive.
2. Director of Naval Intelligence (DNI).

Chapter 2

1. 30 AU used the French Resistance quite often after D-Day.
2. Small operations centres were sometimes necessary for Intelligence officers when writing/compiling reports, as they often had questions for specialists that needed answering/understanding before reports could be completed.
3. 30 AU were split into three main teams – Navy, Royal Marines and Army – and the work was cut up accordingly from there.
4. For further information concerning the detail of 30 AU's remit, the author refers the reader to the *30 Assault Unit User Manual,* Bellac Productions, 2008.
5. Dalzel-Job, Patrick, *Arctic Snow to Dust of Normandy: The Extraordinary Wartime Exploits of a Naval Special Agent*, Pen & Sword, 2005.

Chapter 3

1. From here until the end of Part 1 of this book the unit will be referred to as 30 CU.

Chapter 4

1. At the same time the JPS were creating the D-Day deception, 'Passover', which focused on the Pas de Calais rather than the Normandy beaches.
2. For more information concerning Operation TORCH, Bevan Wheatley and the deception plans, see Chapter XXIII, *Dennis Wheatley – Churchill's Storyteller*, Spellmount, 2006.

Chapter 5

1. See *Ian Fleming's Secret War*, Pen & Sword, 2008.
2. The officers within 30 AU did meet with Fleming and, of course, Godfrey, but rarely the men (see also *Ian Fleming's Secret War*).

Chapter 6

1. Riley flew there on 20 June 1943.
2. BANTAM was an operation that was devised by Lieutenant Commander Curtis and involved a troop monitoring troop movements and reporting their findings back. They would then apprehend a staff car or some such military vehicle and take what intelligence they could from it. Approval was given by the Army but not C-in-C Med who 'did not consider it proper employment for a unit owing allegiances to the RN'. It would have been the first parachute operation for the unit had it been given the final go ahead.

Chapter 10

1. This was communicated to them by their commanding officers and a detailed list of equipment is listed in archives, along with memos etc. written by Fleming concerning 30 CU equipment.
2. Such as Operation TRACER, which ran alongside Fleming's Operation RUTHLESS (see *Ian Fleming's Secret War*).
3. Although it can be argued that the document was published after Godfrey's time, its basic framework was so typical Godfrey and clearly along the lines of his best practice (see previous note).

Chapter 11

1. Largely it would appear, through their having gone into action with soldiers in command, without charts, tide-tables or other guides to navigate.
2. Steinbeck was actually serving with the US Navy as a war correspondent.
3. Two small contingents of British troops were attached to these Italian units.

Chapter 13

1. The garrison of Ishia was strengthened during this period by the arrival of a company of American Airborne Infantry. At the same time Captain J.G. Coates, Intelligence Corps, arrived to join 30 CU from 10 (IA) Commando. Captain Coates was fluent in French, German and Italian and was studying Slovene. He was also a qualified parachutist and had travelled extensively in Europe before the war.
2. The house of the lock-keeper controlled the lock which regulated the flow of water to the reclaimed marshes known as the Licolese.

Chapter 15

1. When one reads any biography concerning Fleming, there is much work conducted by him for his own operations, such as RUTHLESS and GOLDENEYE (and even his potential involvement with the flight of Rudolf Hess) in 1941-2, mainly because Godfrey allowed him to follow through his own plans and give him more freedom than anyone else would. Come 1943, there was much planning for D-Day and Fleming would want some involvement for 30 CU, let alone himself, as he was a very busy secretary to the DNI during this period. Between October and December 1943 – when he got 30 CU home – this was a very frustrating period for the future writer.
2. There is a file note in ADM 223/214 in the National Archive that reads: 'The three officers mentioned and their party had nothing to do in N Africa after Operation BANTUM had been

disallowed and C-in-C Mediterranean, though his staff had indicated that he thought they would be more useful elsewhere. With the approval of Lt Cdr Riley and the knowledge of COHQ, arrangements were accordingly made to C-in-C Mediterranean that they be returned by sea.' That may be so but the happy men were not in the mood for surprise visits, especially when there was already so much lacking in perception and following the rules and protocols that befitted their uniforms. 30 CU was a bit of a headache.

3. This officer was temporarily appointed to the unit by the FMO and was engaged in repairing minor casualties and in promoting the general health of welfare in the men.

4. This action clearly vindicates the fact that DNI saw the worth of 30 CU through their antics – and despite the criticism – good work had been done but the 'mix' hadn't been quite right. There was clearly a problem with the RMs early on and that had to be addressed as a possible upsetting quality within the unit, despite any lessons learnt.

Chapter 16

1. Intelligence planning for the Army Troop was undertaken by Major Cass and later Captain Ward (with some additional support from MI6).

2. The Citadel is a big dark and unsensational building around the back of the Admiralty overlooking St James's Park. It has no windows and today is so overgrown, one is almost forgiven for overlooking the concrete block. It was accessed from deep below the Admiralty and was the operations room for NID 30 (reference to it is made in Patrick Dalzel-Job's autobiography *Arctic Snow to Dust of Normandy*).

3. This document was actually used in the field and was revised once. Veterans told me that the list was a small breast-pocket sized paperback book, not very thick (one resides in a file at the National Archive.)

4. Robert Harling was No. 2 to Lieutenant Donald McLauchlan in NID on the propaganda desk (see *Ian Fleming's Secret War*, Pen & Sword, 2008).

5. Interview conducted for *Ian Fleming's Secret War* and *The History of 30 Assault Unit* by the author at The Marine, Littlehampton, spring 2008.

6. There has been some ambiguity about 30 AU personal weaponry, which is strange because it is so well documented that it included: Fairbairn-Sykes Commando knife, Colt M1911A1 pistol, SMLE No1 MK111, Lee Enfield No 4 rifle, Thompson M1928A1, Sten M1 SMG, Bren MG and Mills grenades. Additional note: the Fairbairn-Sykes Commando Knife (sometimes spelt Fairburn-Sykes, albeit incorrectly) came in three patterns. The first in limited quantities in 1941, the second, specially blackened for UK commandos and a cheaper-looking third version, also blackened. The second pattern usually has 'England' on it and the third pattern either 'England' or 'William Rogers Sheffield England'. It is speculated that most 30 AU commandos had the second pattern, characteristically with ball base, which strangely is sported as a centrepiece to the dust wrapper of the James Bond novel *The Spy Who Loved Me*. Early re-issues of the novel had the silver gilt missing on the indentation of the knife on the front board, possibly at Fleming's request, to fall in line with the blackened commando knife of 30 AU.

7. Dalzel-Job, Patrick, *Arctic Snow to Dust of Normandy*, Pen & Sword, 2005.

Chapter 17

1. Lt Glanville was retained in the Admiralty to work in NID 30, on revising the list of priorities and planning future operations. The other officers returned to the field.

Chapter 18

1. D+4, 10 June 1944, not D+6 as sometimes claimed (see Dalzel-Job, *Arctic Snow to Dust of Norway*).

2. See *Air Defence of Great Britain*, vol. 6 and also *Operation Big Ben: The Anti-V2 Spitfire Missions 1944-45*, Spellmount, 2004.

3. See Danchev, Alex and Todman, Daniel (eds), *War Diaries*

1939-1945, Field Marshal Lord Alanbrooke, Weidenfeld & Nicolson, 2001: 'Last night Germans used their pilotless planes [V1s] for the first time.'
4. Most of this chapter comes from veterans and the autobiography of Patrick Dalzel-Job.

Chapter 20

1. 30 AU did feel that they were the bee's knees. In July 1944 the unit served in Rennes and Brest and then followed Free French Forces into Paris during the liberation of the city in August. They would have acquired many first-hand perceptions from the people they met along the road and formed an opinion effectively based upon Chinese whispers and half-truths.

Annexe A

1. Fleming asked Joan Bright who told him to seek the assistance of somebody like Arthur C. Clarke. Interestingly, Clarke referred to PAPERCLIP scientists briefly in his novel *Childhood's End*. Strangely, Alistair MacLean also referred to PAPERCLIP scientists in *Ice Station Zebra*. So the writers in the know certainly alluded to Operation PAPERCLIP as a significant part of the war effort.

Annexe C

1. Ian was the second eldest of four brothers: Peter, the eldest, worked in British Intelligence; the third, Richard, served in the Lovat Scouts and the Seaforth Highlanders, was wounded and received the Military Cross; and Michael, who died of wounds as a prisoner of the Nazis in 1940.
2. Some people have speculated that Fleming based James Bond on Godfrey. The answer is no, as Donald McLahlan (fellow Room 39 officer) quoted Fleming as stating (see *For Bond Lovers Only*): 'Although he is almost a product of my imagination, I used various people I came across during the war – secret service men, commandos, newspaper men – as a

basis for him. My experiences during the war, and my knowledge of intelligence work led me to write about them in a highly bowdlerized way, and I simply used Bond as a central figure.' The character of M was far more fitting, as both M and Godfrey's last command were on HMS *Repulse* and both shared a taste for Algerian wine.

Sources and Further Reading

ADM 1/15798 Admiralty, and Ministry of Defence, Navy Department, Correspondence and Papers.
Foreign Countries (53): Operation WOOLFORCE: reports of activities of No. 30 Assault Unit in Paris 1944.

ADM 199/2488 Admiralty: War History Cases and Papers. Second World War. Director of Navy Intelligence ... 30 Assault Unit documents and duplicates of port war damage information, including CX information.

ADM 202/308 Admiralty and Ministry of Defence: Royal Marines: war diaries, unit diaries, detachment reports and orders.
30 Assault Unit, Admiralty and Ministry of Defence.

ADM 202/598 Admiralty and Ministry of Defence.
30 Assault Unit: Photographs, vol. 1.
World War II. Advance on Cherbourg. Surrender to 30 Assault Unit, Royal Marines, or Naval headquarters personnel. Prisoners emerge from tunnel at Octeville, 26 June.

ADM 202/599 Admiralty and Ministry of Defence.
30 Assault Unit, vol. 2: war diaries, unit diaries and detachment reports.

ADM 223/213 Admiralty: Navy Intelligence Division and

Operational Intelligence Centre: intelligence reports and papers. Appendix 1 (part 5): History of SIGINT operations undertaken by 30 Commando/30 Assault Unit.

ADM 223/214 Appendix 1 (part 5): History of 30 Commando (later called 30 Assault Unit and 30 Advanced Unit also known as Special Engineering Unit): includes part played by Commander Ian Fleming, Operation TORCH (North Africa), Dieppe Raid, Operation BANTAM (Calabria).

ADM 223/500 30 Assault Unit (formally Special Engineering Unit) and 30 Commando: papers, including field information agency, and technical and correspondence with Commander Ian Fleming, intelligence information and capture of weapons required for Operation OVERLORD (Normandy).

ADM 202/598 30 Assault Unit: photographs, vol 1. 30 Assault Unit: photographs, vol. 1, Admiralty and Ministry of Defence.

ADM 202/599 30 Assault Unit, vol. 2. 30 Assault Unit, vol. 2, Admiralty and Ministry of Defence.

ADM 223/480 Admiralty: Naval Intelligence Division and Operational Intelligence Centre. Reports and papers.
U-boat supply ships at Cape Verde. Rubble (special steels and machine tools) contracts in Sweden ... correspondence with Commander Ian Fleming.

ADM 223/490 Admiralty: Naval Intelligence Division and Operational Intelligence Centre. Intelligence reports and papers. Spain (including North Africa territories) and Portugal. Includes Goldeneye (precautions against German invasion of Spain) and correspondence with Commander Ian Fleming.

ADM 223/2 Admiralty Intelligence Papers.

ADM 223/3 Admiralty Intelligence Papers 1941-42.

ADM 223/349 Admiralty: Naval Intelligence Division and Operational Intelligence Centre: intelligence and reports.
No. 30 Assault Unit: targets lists for operations in Germany (second edition).

ADM 223/501 Admiralty: Navy Intelligence Division and Operational Intelligence Centre: Intelligence Reports and Papers.
30 Assault Unit targets. Admiralty … reports and papers NID Volumes.

Box 4 ACH/4 African Coastal Flotilla: mostly research notes about units' operations during Second World War.

DEDE 2/1107 Combined Operations Headquarters, and Ministry of Defence … Amphibious Warfare Headquarters.
30 Assault Unit (formally Special Engineering Unit, formally 30 Command, later 30 Advanced Unit): mobilization, control, disbandment, honours and awards.

HW 8/104 Government Code and Cypher School: Naval Section: Reports, Working Aids and Correspondence.
History of 30 Commando (latterly called 30 Assault Unit and 30 Advance Unit) including History of SIGINT operations undertaken by 30 Commando/30 AU. This is a detailed account of wartime operations conducted by 30 Commando to obtain enemy documents and equipment.

WO219/1160 War Office: Supreme Headquarters … 30 Assault Unit: miscellaneous cables…

ADM 223/214 Official history of 30 Assault Unit and 'Intelligence Assault Force Operations': an A5 booklet detailing how to create such a unit.

(The further reading titles listed below are those used in research for this book, not necessarily the first editions)

Braddon, Russell, *Cheshire VC*, Evans Brothers Ltd, 1954.

Dalzel-Job, Patrick, *Arctic Snow to Dust of Normandy: The Extraordinary Wartime Exploits of a Naval Special Agent*, Pen & Sword, 2005.

Danchev, Alex and Todman, Daniel (eds), *War Diaries 1939-1945, Field Marshal Lord Alanbrooke*, Weidenfeld & Nicolson, 2001.

Fleming, Ian, *Moonraker*, Cape, 1955.

Lewis, John, *Jock Lewis, Co-founder of the SAS*, Leo Cooper, 2000.

McLachlan, Donald, *Room 39*, Weidenfeld & Nicolson, 1968.

Middlebrook, Martin and Everitt, Chris, *The Bomber Command War Diaries: An Operational Reference Book, 1939-1945*, Viking, 1985.

Nutting, David (ed.), *Attain by Surprise*, David Colver Publisher, 1997.

The Memoirs of Field Marshal the Viscount Montgomery of Alamein, KG, Collins, 1958.

Index

THE HISTORY OF
30 ASSAULT UNIT

Ian Fleming's Red Indians

Books by Craig Cabell

Frederick Forsyth – A Matter of Protocol, the Authorised Biography
The Kray Brothers – The Image Shattered
James Herbert – Devil in the Dark, the Authorised True Story
Operation Big Ben – the anti-V2 Spitfire Missions 1944-45 (with Graham. A. Thomas)
VE Day – A Day to Remember (with Allan Richards)
Snipers (with Richard Brown)
Dennis Wheatley – Churchill's Storyteller
Getting Away With Murder (with Lenny Hamilton)
Witchfinder General – the Biography of Matthew Hopkins
Ian Fleming's Secret War – Author of James Bond
The Hunt for Captain Kidd (with Graham A. Thomas & Allan Richards)
The Hunt for Blackbeard (with Graham A. Thomas & Allan Richards)
The History of 30 Assault Unit – Ian Fleming's Red Indians
Ian Rankin and Inspector Rebus

(Chap Books)
Dennis Wheatley and the Occult
Black Sniper (fiction)
I was Alive Then – The Spike Milligan Interviews
The Grapes of MoD – ten years of wine consumption
30 Assault Unit User Manual
Dennis Wheatley's Total War
The Curse of the Bakervilles
William – The Story of a Royal Marine
Robert Heinlein Complete UK Bibliography

(Special Introductions)
Furies Over Korea – the story of the men of the Fleet Air Arm, RAF and Commonwealth who defended South Korea, 1950-1953, by Graham A. Thomas
Firestorm, Typhoons Over Caen, 1944 by Graham A. Thomas
Terror from the Sky – the Battle Against the Flying Bomb by Graham A. Thomas